William Dudley Foulke

Slav or Saxon

A Study of the Growth and Tendencies of Russian Civilization

William Dudley Foulke

Slav or Saxon
A Study of the Growth and Tendencies of Russian Civilization

ISBN/EAN: 9783337400040

Printed in Europe, USA, Canada, Australia, Japan

Cover: Foto ©ninafisch / pixelio.de

More available books at **www.hansebooks.com**

QUESTIONS OF THE DAY. No. XLIII.

SLAV OR SAXON

A STUDY OF THE GROWTH AND TENDENCIES OF
RUSSIAN CIVILIZATION

BY

WILLIAM DUDLEY FOULKE

SECOND EDITION, REVISED

G. P. PUTNAM'S SONS
NEW YORK AND LONDON
The Knickerbocker Press
1898

PREFACE TO SECOND EDITION.

THE certainty of the coming conflict between the Slav and the Saxon, which was foreshadowed in the edition of this work published in 1887, has become more generally apparent during the past year, owing to Russian intrigues in China; while the cordial friendship between England and America, which has grown up during our war with Spain, has made possible the union of American and English influence for the protection of our common civilization against the encroachments of autocracy.

The time therefore seems opportune for issuing a revised edition, bringing down to the present moment the existing facts relating to the coming struggle, a struggle which seems certain to involve in its results the destiny of the whole human race.

W. D. F.

RICHMOND, IND., Dec. 1, 1898.

AMONG the publications to which I have been under obligations, are " L' Empire des Tsars et les Russes," by Anatole Leroy-Beaulieu; Rambaud's " History of Russia "; Stepniak's " Russia under the Tsars," " Underground Russia," and " The Russian Storm Cloud "; Vámbéry's articles in the *Nineteenth Century* entitled " Will Russia Conquer India ? "; " The Russians at the Gates of Herat," by Charles Marvin; Tissot's " Russes et Allemands," Wallace's " Russia," and Dixon's " Free Russia "; also " China in Transformation," by A. R. Colquhoun, and the recent articles of Stanley, Hallett, Younghusband, and others in the *Nineteenth Century*. The literature upon the subject is comprehensive, and I have drawn freely from many sources, but more especially from the foregoing.

CONTENTS.

SLAV OR SAXON.

CHAPTER I.

THE COMING STRUGGLE.

IT was said in an article published in the *St. Petersburg Novoë Vremya*, in the year 1886, that Mr. Gladstone had recently uttered these words : " I like Russia, not without reason. I recognize in her a true and logical ally of England. The vital resources of the states of Europe are rapidly becoming exhausted. Their bone and sinew are going to Asia, Africa, and America. But long experience proves that there are only two nations who know how to colonize—England and Russia. The other nations totally lack this quality. Therefore England and Russia only have a future. The other powers are on the decline. The time is not far off when Germany and France will disappear from the horizon of first-class powers. I hold, therefore, that it is bad policy for England and Russia to quarrel. Let us look at the question from the standpoint of mere profit. Where are the principal interests of Russia? In the Balkan Peninsula. And ours? In India and Africa. Therefore we might easily and advantageously to both, draw our limits.   We prefer Russia as an ally, also, because she has already land enough to last her for centuries.   Russia is the most powerful country on land, and England is the most powerful country on sea.   In this difference there is a mutual guaranty of our friendship."

Whether Mr. Gladstone said these things or not, the thought that England and Russia are to be the two great nations of the Old World, is one which must have occurred to those who have watched the development of the great Northern power, and contrasted it with the growth of Anglo-Saxon civilization and with that of the remainder of continental Europe.   The only mistake is the belief that the Slav and the Anglo-Saxon can continue to colonize and to conquer without collision.   These two great branches of the Aryan stock, so different in character, customs, political life, and modes of thought, will never hold in harmony the divided sovereignty of the Eastern Continent.   The deep-seated jealousy and ill-will which England and Russia show toward each other, have a basis more logical than the conclusions of Mr. Gladstone; and sooner or later must come that struggle for dominion which shall determine whether the civilization of the Slav or that of the Saxon shall be the civilization of the world.

It is not easy for us in America to realize the gravity of the crisis.   The nearness of our own forms of civilization shuts out from view the growth of the type which is more distant, or if we see it, we do not allow enough for the perspective.   Russia is a long way off.   Her ideas are so outlandish, so semi-barbarous, so undesirable in every way, according to our thinking, that we do not see how they can be forced down the throat of humanity. Our own forms of social life are so much higher and better, that we feel sure that they must ultimately survive.

But although the law of the survival of the fittest prevails in social, as well as in organic life, this does not always mean the survival of the highest type. In animal life many highly developed organisms have disappeared, while some of the simplest and crudest types exist to-day. So in history we find that many intellectual races have fallen a prey to barbarians. No one would have believed in the Rome of the Antonines, that the stretch of her universal empire would be invaded, her legions overthrown, and her civilization all but extinguished by the half-naked and undisciplined hordes of Germany and Scythia, that same Scythia which is now creeping stealthily into the Balkan peninsula, China, and the plains of Central Asia; no one would have dreamed that the wealth and refinement of mediæval India would become a prey to the wild tribes of Tartary, that same Tartary through which Russia to-day is working her way for another and more lasting conquest. The history of Russia herself furnishes several instances of high types of liberalism and culture, trodden down and stamped out by the brute force of barbarism. The Khazarui, a liberal and enlightened people of the South of Russia, who in the Middle Ages maintained intimate relations with Byzantium and Bagdad and Cordova, who built great cities, who established flourishing schools, who tolerated all religions, were crushed out and swept away by the barbarous peoples around them. It is, then, no answer to say that because Russian culture is inferior to that of the Anglo-Saxon, that the Russian race must go under in the struggle. The question is this: does Russia possess those conditions of physical force which insure its future supremacy? The characteristics of the land, and of the race which inhabits it, furnish great food for thought.

First of all, it is evident enough, as Mr. Gladstone says, that among the nations of the Eastern Continent, England and Russia only have a future. The diminutive area of the remainder of continental Europe is not large enough to grow in. No people can acquire a lasting supremacy who are pent up within boundaries as narrow as those of any country in Western Europe. Indeed, we can see everywhere, except in England, America, and Russia, signs that the limits of growth are not far off. Leaving out of the question all mere barbarous communities, and those smaller peoples whose national unity is scarcely strong enough to protect them from the aggressions of their neighbors; passing by such forms of nationality as the Ottoman and Persian empires, which are visibly tottering to ruin, or the Chinese, crystallized for centuries and now crumbling to pieces, we come to types like those furnished by the Latin races. Take Spain, for example. Spain grew with marvellous rapidity. It was but a lifetime from the anarchy which preceded the reign of Ferdinand and Isabella to the great empire of Charles V.; but under the influence of a baleful ecclesiasticism, the work of decay was as rapid as that of growth. Spain had a boundless empire in the New World, and she tried to colonize, but failed. The elements of progress were wanting, disintegration began, one colony after another dropped away, the defects of the parent stock repeated themselves in the offspring, and in the Spanish-American colonies, with new land and new political institutions, we have the early decrepitude inherited with Spanish blood. In Spain itself every thing reminds us of past greatness and present weakness. It is a land of memory, not of hope.

There is reason to believe that France has seen its best days. That nation has played a brilliant part in history. The warlike instincts of the people, their keenness of intellect, their nervous energy, the elegance of their manners, their high rank in all that pertains to material civilization, the progress of their liberal thought, and their present republican institutions, show little signs of decay. Yet the French people of to-day are physically inferior to their ancestors. The wars of Napoleon made terrible ravages with their best types of manhood, while the prevalent licentiousness which is ingrained in their literature as well as in their lives, gives us reason to believe that the French are not growing. They do not assimilate well with other peoples. They cannot colonize. In Canada, in Louisiana, in Hindostan, in the West Indies, they failed. Will they succeed better in Africa, Tongking, and Madagascar? Where are the colonists to people these new possessions? French conquests are not permanent. The territory of France to-day is less than that of ancient Gaul. The population does not grow. It may well be that the downward step taken in the war with Germany was but the beginning of the end.

The great problem of Italian unity having been solved,
that kingdom showed new signs of life ; but it is not a
first-class power, and there is no indication that its vitality
will extend much beyond the peninsula which it occupies.
It is limited, like France and Germany, by natural boundaries, both of territory and race.

There is probably no great nation in the world whose
life hangs upon a slenderer thread than that of Austria.
Composed of a number of widely different races, there
seems to be a lack of the power of welding them together,
and the very existence of the monarchy is continually
threatened with the possible disruption of its incongruous
parts. Possessing, like France and Germany, a territory
easily invaded, the most that can be expected is that it
will retain, for a limited time only, its present status.
During this generation, it has been stripped of its hegem-
ony in the German Confederation and of its Italian
possessions, and has obtained but a poor compensation in the control of semi-barbarous Bosnia. The Austrian dynasty is the oldest in Europe, and the nation, if
nation it can be called, betrays, most plainly of all, the
weaknesses of old age.

Germany, of late, has made great strides toward power
and leadership in Europe. The patience and high intellectual attainments of the German people, the admirable organization of the German army, and the genius of
the Great Chancellor, placed it for a time at the head
of Continental nations. But Germany has not yet shown
any ability to leap across ethnological barriers. Its territory, situated in the heart of Europe, and densely

peopled, does not furnish any great natural facilities for repelling aggressions, and the Germans do not colonize. The system of "the balance of power," so long recognized in Europe, will not permit the conquest of adjoining nations by Germany *ad libitum*. It will not allow the growth of the German people much faster than by natural multiplication. The density of population is such, that this growth will press too closely upon subsistence to be very great. Much of the best blood of Germany is passing to America to be absorbed by us. There is reason to think that German power is not far from its culmination ; there is certainly a near limit, beyond which it cannot pass. The Germans themselves seem to be conscious of this. We can see this feeling in their late efforts to drive the wedge of colonization into the Carolines, the Samoan Islands, Africa, New Guinea, China,—anywhere to give themselves more room. But they can only colonize by sea, and there Great Britain holds them at her mercy. The limits of German expansion have been fixed by an inexorable law.

The three great peoples that remain are the Americans, the English, and the Russians. All three have this common advantage : they have unlimited facilities for growth. They can extend their dominions either by conquest or peaceful colonization into parts of the world where it will not be limited by the jealousy and balance-of-power statesmanship of neighboring peoples. They have not only the physical ability to grow, but they have also an inherent capacity for colonizing. The progress of the United States has been rapid, but our activity has been limited to the Western Continent. We are happily freed by our unquestionable supremacy in America from those international struggles which distract the other hemisphere, and we can move along in the paths of our internal development with little fear of foreign interference or invasion. But the Eastern Continent possesses twice the area and nearly ten times the population of the Western. The struggle for the supremacy of the world must be fought there, and the great colossi who will contest it with each other are England and Russia. The future world is to be Slav or Saxon.

This struggle is coming sooner than it would seem, if we compare it with the slow development of nations and races in the past. Not that we shall live to see it ; it may be generations ahead of us, but the rapidity of social changes to-day is as much greater than that of like changes in past ages, as the speed of the locomotive is greater than that of the coach or caravan. We are scarcely yet able to realize the gigantic strides which civilization has made within our own times. We do as much now in ten years as the ancient world did in a thousand. If we look over the map of our boyhood, we can hardly recognize it. Take our own country. We used to see an enormous tract called the " Great American Desert." Whither has it gone? The vast blank on the map of Central Africa, that was marked " unexplored "—what has become of it ? We see a network of innumerable railways, over prairies which were then unknown. A ship canal is soon to unite the Atlantic and Pacific, as one already joins the Indian Ocean with the Mediterranean. The time was when it took a century to civilize a tribe, a thousand years to develop a province. Now a single generation will witness the transformation of a whole continent.

The great struggle between the Slav and the Saxon is not very far away. Its coming is already faintly visible. We see nothing now but a cloud the size of a man's hand, but the air is pregnant with a storm which will darken the whole sky. The difficulties in Afghanistan, Bulgaria, and China are only faint premonitory murmurs; the real evidence of the coming struggle is the massing of the social forces on either side. There may be a dozen conflicts, followed by a dozen reconciliations; they would mean little except for the vast powers looming up behind.

Let us review these marshalling forces and see whether the picture is overdrawn, or the danger is overestimated. Let us look at the future of England and Russia, in the light of what we know of their past. Let us examine the resources of the empire of the Czars, in respect to territory, population, wealth, military appliances, and other material and intellectual advantages and deficiencies. Let us look at the growth of Russia and see, if we can, whither its future tends.

CHAPTER II.

THE TERRITORY OF RUSSIA.

IN the matter of land, Russia possesses nearly one sixth of the entire world, and her territory is continually growing larger by conquest and colonization. Her possessions are greater in extent than those of any other nation that exists to-day, or any which has ever existed. With the gradual filling up of the world, this question of land is becoming more and more important. The mere quantity of earth seems to be the only thing which remains constant. If there be only space enough, the same skill which redeemed Holland from the sea, which consigned the Great American Desert to the realms of imagination, which built St. Petersburg upon a marsh, and Archangel upon the shores of the Frozen Ocean, seems able everywhere to transmute that space into a productive agent for supplying the wants of man. The most inhospitable rock yields ore of priceless value. The swamp and bog contain the choicest soil; the very Arctic teems with exhaustless life. Sahara itself needs nothing but the enterprise and skill of future generations to be transformed into a garden. So long as a nation grows, the value of its land continues to increase. The time has been when the richest soil of Russia had no value. The time may come when the plains of Turkestan and the forests of Siberia will be valuable as the fields of Central Russia are to-day. Formerly great extent of territorial possessions was an element of political weakness. The forces of the state were scattered over a wide region where communication was impossible. When a province was attacked, it took too long to hear from it, too long to send assistance. By the time thought was interchanged, the conditions were all different.

The Emperor Adrian relinquished vast provinces because it weakened Rome to defend them. But now in a week we can make the journey of a year; in the transmission of thought, space is annihilated altogether. The extent of its territory is the strongest security of Russian despotism; it prevents opposing forces from concentrating, while the central authority, which controls the avenues of communication, can speedily bring its whole force to bear upon a single point anywhere in its dominions.

Not only does the Russian Empire stand pre-eminent in mere extent of territory, it is equally remarkable for the homogeneity of its possessions. "Its principal characteristic is unity in immensity." Western Europe is broken by mountain ranges and divided by seas, gulfs, and bays; there is diversity everywhere. Commerce is largely external, agriculture is of every kind, natural barriers separate great countries like Spain, England, Scandinavia, and Italy from the rest. But the Europe of Russia is one vast plain. The same physical unity prevails in Siberia and Turkestan. "Russia in Asia is not an exotic colony

impossible to assimilate or difficult to keep. It is a
prolongation and natural dependence of the European
territories."

The monotony and level character of the land is not
with out its influence upon the temperament of the people.
The lack of originality and individuality noticed by
travellers in Russia is partly due to this cause.   From an
industrial point of view this unity has its disadvantages ;
the employments of the people are not diversified. Russia
is too much an agricultural state.   But from a political
point of view nothing could be better adapted to the concentration of power.   The people become a unit like the
land, their occupations are the same, their thoughts, their
aspirations.   They are much more easily subjected to the
control of a single will.   Their separate interests are not
blowing toward every quarter like the winds from the
cave of Eolus.

There is, however, one great variety in nature—the
change of the seasons.   It is only a few weeks from
the bitter cold of an arctic winter to the heat of a
summer which is more than tropical.   The transformation of nature is brilliant and startling.   The winters
are dazzling, the nights of summer are one long twi-
light.   The peasants' songs of spring, which celebrate
the arrival of the " birds from paradise," the harvest
melodies, which have for their theme the sudden ripening of the grain, and the songs of autumn, lamenting the
departure of all fruitfulness in nature, are evidences of the
effect upon the Russian temperament of these transforma-
tions.   The flexibility of Russian character owes much to

these sudden changes. If they lack originality in intellect, there is great originality in their feelings, tastes, and habits. The innumerable sects of religious fanatics, the strange types of character of which Ivan the Terrible and Peter the Great are illustrations, the capacity of the Russians for tremendous efforts upon occasions rather than for sustained endeavor, are not without relation to their long winters of torpor and inactivity, and their short, burning summers, when the work of a year must be compressed into a few brief months. To this, in part, may also be due the twofold character remarked by students of Russian life, the excesses of liberalism and conservatism, of veneration and cynicism, of hope and despondency, of intelligence and ignorance; the boldness in projects of reform, the timidity in execution. These contradictions, however, are modified by the practical good-sense of the Russians, their tendency to realism rather than abstract thought, their leaning toward physical science rather than intellectual philosophy. In all these things the nation shows the impulses and tendencies of childhood, and further culture and development may correct its shortcomings. The desire for reforms of a tangible and physical nature remind one much of the same tendency among our own people. With greater education and more liberty the Russians would hardly be behind us in this respect.

The introduction of steam for travel and transportation will give greater advantages to Russia than to any other country. Its weakness in early days was its want of access to the sea. It was to remedy this that Peter the

Great conquered the Baltic provinces and built St. Petersburg. It was in great part for this that he and Catharine
and Nicholas plotted to overthrow the Ottoman Empire,
to gain possession of the Bosphorus. But in these latter
days, when communication by land is easier and swifter
than by sea, this disadvantage is scarcely felt. From her
present position Russia could overrun the whole Eastern
Continent without a navy. For the purposes of international, as well as internal commerce, the railroad will soon
supersede the ship and the steamer. In a struggle between
England and Russia the maritime supremacy of England
would be of little avail.

Not only has Russia a vast extent of dominion, but a
considerable portion of her territory is the most fertile
land in the world. Across European Russia extend, from
Northeast to Southwest, three great belts—the forests, the
black land, and the steppes. Over the entire North of
Russia extend these great forests. Many of the oldest
cities have been built in the clearings. In the extreme
North the land is barren, elsewhere it is fairly productive.
South of the forests comes the great belt of black land.
There is no richer soil anywhere. It has been farmed for
centuries without fertilization ; but the most ruinous system of agriculture has failed to weaken its powers. " A
little rest," as the farmers call it, has been all that has
been needed. South of the black land extend the
steppes, the prairies of Russia, where the grass grows
higher than men's heads. The Northern part of these
prairies is also fertile ; to the South they are adapted to
pasturage only. The barren lands were formerly the

depths of a great inland sea. The area of this district is much less than that of the fertile steppes.

These great belts are prolonged into Siberia. In the early history of Russia the South line of the forests was the boundary line which divided the agricultural from the nomad population, the Russians from the Tartars, the Muscovites from the Cossacks. In the forests, the population grows more slowly than farther South, and the peasants add to their farming a great variety of little industries in their agricultural villages, in which they engage during the long winter when there can be no labor in the field. More fruitful in agricultural promise are the unwooded zones of the South, which are increased from year to year by the cutting away of the forests.

The black land and the Northern steppes, like our basin of the Mississippi, constitute one of those great storehouses of grain which seem to guarantee an unlimited supply for the future. The fertile steppes, like our prairies, are a vast sea of verdure, which is gradually falling into the hands of the husbandmen. It is destined to be conquered, by the peasants until " the steppes of Gogol, as in America the prairies of Cooper, will soon be nothing but a remembrance."

During thousands of years, the great migrations from Asia into Europe have passed across these plains, and until the present century, the steppes have remained exposed to the encroachments of nomads. The settlement of much of the best land in Russia has been thus delayed. It has been since the subjugation of the Crimean Tartars and the Kirghis of the Caspian that this vast region has become secure for the development of systematic agriculture. Two natural obstacles remain—the absence of trees and the great dryness of the climate. But the discovery of oil and coal in these regions, and the improved facilities for commerce, are soon to furnish the steppes of Russia with sufficient fuel and building material, while the planting of trees, which is even now commenced in some places, is likely to overcome the seasons of barrenness occasioned by the excessive drought.

The present system of agriculture is very wasteful. Large tracts are abandoned successively every few years by the communities that farm them in most primitive fashion. But this is an evil which improved methods of culture are already beginning to overcome.

The mineral resources of Russia are almost wholly undeveloped, though we know that rich mines of gold, silver, lead, copper, and platinum lie hidden in the depths of the Ural and Altai mountains. These regions seem destined to open up a new civilization in the same way as California and Australia.

At a time when water-power was so essential to manufactures, Russia was behindhand in this great department of industry; but now that steam has usurped the place of this old motive-power, her advantages are equal to any. In natural facilities for agriculture, commerce, and manufactures, as well as in mineral resources, Russia is not inferior to the most favored nations. Her natural productions render her wholly self-sustaining. If the ports of every civilized nation were closed against her, Russia would feel the loss less than any country in the world.

In this, too, we see a great advantage in a military point of view.

There is some drawback in the matter of climate ; the whole of Russia and Siberia is subject to intense cold in winter. The heat of summer is scarcely less intense ; the climate has great extremes. The Northern plains of Siberia, stretching away into the Arctic Circle, as well as a considerable portion of Northern Russia, seem uninhabitable. In the whole North the period of vegetation is shorter, and the product of the earth more limited on that account. It looks to us now as though a great part of Russia must always remain a waste. But it is probable that we little know the powers of the civilization of the future for utilizing the most dreary and barren regions. The ancient world would never have dreamed that a great city could be built on the shores of the White Sea. Russia has one compensation for this climate : It has produced a race, hardy, patient, and energetic ; the only civilized beings who can endure the rigors of its dreadful winters. The perseverance of Russian colonists and soldiers in overcoming obstacles which would be insurmountable to others, has long been recognized by the world.

Herbert Spencer says that the earliest civilization began in warm countries, where men did not have to wrestle with the elements for life alone ; where there was some surplus energy for the formation of society ; but that as civilization went on, and as the means of overcoming natural objects became greater, the highest social development moved into colder regions, where natural ob-

stacles brought out a corresponding energy, which not
only overcame them, but strengthened the type. It is
rather Northward than Westward that the course of empire moves; beginning in India, Egypt, and Carthage, it
has crept gradually up to Greece, Rome, Spain, France,
till the sceptre passed to England, as it is now passing to
Russia. The reign of the Normans in Sicily, France,
England, and Russia itself, attests the supremacy of
Northern vigor.

The very fruitfulness of nature is sometimes hostile to
the development of mankind. " Russia," in the words of
Leroy-Beaulieu, " while it is ill-fitted to nourish the infancy of civilization, is one of those countries which is admirably adapted to receive it and give it further growth."
" The Russian soil does not use as its mere instrument
him who cultivates it. It does not threaten his race with
degeneration. It makes no creoles. Man meets there
only two obstructions—cold and space. Cold, more easily
overcome than extreme heat and less to be feared by our
civilization ; space, an enemy already mastered by Russia
and its great ally for the future."

The great extent of its territory, the sternness of its
climate, and the absence of large centres of population,
make a conquest of the country all but impossible. Russia can be invaded, many of its towns destroyed, and perhaps, even its capital taken; but the patience of a people
who are willing to sacrifice their homes at the command
of their emperor, to submit and to suffer as long as it
may be necessary, and who alone are able to endure the
rigors of a Russian winter, is sufficient to secure the

ultimate annihilation of any army which attempts the sudden conquest of Russia. There is too much of it to overrun. Nature combines with man to exterminate the invader.

The only manner in which this vast empire could ever be subdued or reduced to an inferior position, is the manner in which Russia has herself spread her dominion, that is by the conquest in detail of small portions of her immense possessions (for instance, the Baltic Provinces, Poland, or Finland); the conqueror gradually consolidating his power in the conquered provinces. This would require not only superior strength, but a persistent purpose, extending over many years and probably generations. What nation is in a condition to undertake so vast an enterprise ?

CHAPTER III.

THE RUSSIAN PEOPLE.

THE present population of the Russian empire is about one hundred and twenty-five millions. That of the British empire, embracing the dense masses of India and Africa, is about four hundred millions. But the strength of a nation is not to be reckoned by mere numbers. The population of the Chinese empire is the greatest in the world, yet its solid and lifeless mass cannot resist the most trifling aggressions. The Indian empire of Her Majesty is composed of material of much the same sort. The soldiery has been greatly improved by European training, but it is still far behind that of Russia in those patient and enduring qualities which offer the only assurance of success in a long and desperate struggle.

The population of Russia is distributed very unevenly. In the North and South it is extremely sparse; in the centre it is comparatively dense. This comprises the southern part of the forest zone, the black land, and Poland. Here manufactures and other branches of industry are most fully developed. The centre of gravity of population is near Moscow—a little to the South of the ancient capital. In the central districts it is nearly as dense as in continental Europe, and it grows most rapidly in these places.

The Russian race is a compound of many elements, welded and fused together, sometimes by the most violent means. This process is still going on among the frontier races, especially among the Asiatic peoples. These are first conquered and then absorbed. The orginal stock, the Slav, which has retained the predominance in this work of compounding and re-compounding, belongs to the great Aryan family. Its kinship to the races of West Europe is shown by its language as well as by its physical and intellectual traits. The Slavs are most closely connected with the Germans in language, but they are nearer the Greeks and Latins in character. They are mobile, enthusiastic, intelligent, quick to perceive and act; they lack the phlegmatic temperament of the Teutonic race. They are the latest grown of the Aryan children. Even to-day they are not sufficiently developed to reveal fully their intellectual aptitudes. Their country was exposed to continual Asiatic incursions, in past times, and their growth and civilization were greatly retarded. It is only in our generation that they have begun to assume any intellectual prominence; but those who are acquainted with the Russian literature of the present time, with the masterpieces of Tolstoi, Turgeneff, and Gogol, will hardly fail to foresee a brilliant future for a people capable of producing such works. Among the branches of the Aryan stock, those later in civilization have successively asserted their superiority over their elder brethren. The Greek yielded to

the Roman, the Roman to the Teuton and the Anglo-
Saxon, and it is not beyond the bounds of possibility that
even these may in turn give way to the Slav.   Up to the
present time the Slav peoples have been thought to lack
originality.   They have been learners at the schools of
more enlightened nations, but their present literature
shows that they are by no means wanting in the higher
qualities of intellect.

The parent people took up their abode in Western
Russia, at an early day, while other branches of the
same stock in Poland, Moravia, Bulgaria, Croatia, Servia,
Bohemia, and elsewhere, became the ancestors of many of
the various peoples now subject to Austrian and German
rule, and of some that dwell in the Balkan Peninsula in
a chaotic and unstable condition of semi-independence.
There was also, at an early period, a small infusion of
Byzantine blood, together with a large infusion of Byzantine influence, and later, some admixture with Teutonic
stock, especially in the Baltic provinces ; also an amalgamation with the Lithuanians, an ancient Aryan race,
who preserved their primitive habits and their pagan-
ism to a late period.   But the great bulk of the tribes
and races which the Slavs have absorbed were of Mongolian or Turanian origin.   Most important among these
during the early process of amalgamation, were the innumerable Finnish tribes.   Nestor, the oldest historian of
Russia, gives us such a multitude of names of strange
peoples which have disappeared from history, that it con-
fuses us.   Gradually these races were absorbed ; a few
remnants are all that tell us where the rest have gone.

Then came the fusion with Turks and Tartars, each change strengthening the Slav stock, while many of the Mongolian characteristics faded away. The Slavs of Great Russia (the Eastern portion surrounding Moscow) · became gradually predominant and multiplied most rapidly. It was they who acquired (mostly from the Finns, but also in part from the Tartars) the largest share of Mongolian blood. The Slavs of White Russia in the West, and Little Russia farther South, of purer ancestry, remained subordinate and increased more slowly. Russian and Pole were once of the same race. Differences in religion and habits of political thought, during several centuries, have made the Poles the most intractable among the subjects of the Czar.

The work of fusion, which has been going on for centuries, has thus developed the present Great Russian nationality, which now comprises a majority of the subjects of the Czar, and forms the ethnical basis of the Russian Empire. This process of race change and amalgamation is still going on at points farther removed from the centre of the empire. Even the savages of Eastern Siberia are gradually being Russianized. Russian colonists go everywhere, mingle with the original peoples, and soon absorb them. There are to-day some eighty different races of men subject to the autocrat; races that speak every possible language; races that come from every parent stock; races of every religion—Buddhists, Lamäists, Jews, Protestants, Greeks, Catholics, Mohammedans, and pagans of many varieties; peoples that follow every pursuit in life—savages and nomads,

as well as pastoral, agricultural, and industrial communities.

But, in the language of Leroy-Beaulieu:

With all its diverse races, Russia is by no means an inco-
herent mass, a sort of political conglomerate or marqueterie
of peoples. It resembles rather France than Turkey or
Austria in the matter of national unity. If Russia can be
compared to a mosaic, it is one of those ancient pavements
where the basis is of a single substance and a single color,
whose surface only is made of an embroidery of different
pieces and diverse colors. The greater part of the population
of foreign origin is thrown out on the extremities of Russia
and forms around her, especially toward the East and West, a
sort of girdle of greater or less thickness. All the centre is
filled by a nationality, at once absorbing and expansive, in the
midst of which are hidden some small German colonies and
weak Finnish or Tartar communities, without coherence or
national bond. In the interior of Russia, in place of unlike-
nesses, varieties, and contrasts, that which strikes the traveller
is the uniformity of population and the monotony of life.

The language has few dialects, the towns are of the
same form, the peasants the same in habits and mode of
life. "The nation is made in the image of nature; it
shows the same unity, almost the same monotony, as the
plains which it inhabits."

The tendency to colonize and incorporate other races
is aided by a remarkable physical peculiarity of Russia.
Throughout the whole of its great central plain, stone is
almost entirely absent ; the buildings are generally of
wood. Dwellings of this kind do not last. It used to

be said that the towns of Russia were burned once every seven years. This lack of permanence, together with the vast supply of land and the absence of natural barriers, made the people half nomadic. Formerly, great bodies of peasants would leave their farms and start together in search of better lands. This tendency to move on still remains a trait of the Russian people. It is the parent spirit of that enterprise which is to-day civilizing the forests of Siberia and the plains of Turkestan. Russia belongs to one of those races which has been driven to continual motion by an impulse from within, one of those races whose calling is emigration and conquest. Rambaud, in his history of Russia, describes the process very forcibly. He says:

We must recognize that the Russian, almost as much as the Anglo-Saxon, has the instinct which drives men to emigrate and found colonies. The Russians do, in the far East of Europe, what the Anglo-Saxons do in the far West of America. They belong to one of the great races of pioneers and back-woodsmen. All the history of the Russian people, from the foundation of Moscow, is that of their advance into the forest, into the black land, into the prairie. The Russian has his trappers and settlers in the Cossacks of the Dnieper, the Don, and the Terek ; in the tireless fur-hunters of Siberia ; in the gold-diggers of the Ural and the Altai ; in the adventurous monks who lead the way, founding in regions ever more distant, a monastery which is to be the centre of a town ; lastly, in the Raskolniki, or Dissenters, Russian Puritans or Mormons, who are persecuted by laws human and divine, and seek from forest to forest the Jerusalem of their dreams.

The level plains of Russia naturally tempted men to migration. The mountain keeps her own, the mountain calls her wanderers to return ; while the steppe, stretching away to the dimmest horizon, invites you to advance, to ride at a venture, to "go where the eyes glance." The flat and monotonous soil has no hold on its inhabitants ; they will find as bare a landscape anywhere. As for their hovel, how can they care for that, it is burned down so often ? The Western expression, "the ancestral roof," has no meaning for the Russian peasant. The native of Great Russia, accustomed to live on little, and endure the extremes of heat and cold, was born to brave the dangers and privations of the emigrant's life. With his crucifix, his ax in his belt, and his boots slung behind his back, he will go to the end of the Eastern world. However weak may be the infusion of the Russian element in an Asiatic population, it cannot transmute itself or disappear ; it must become the dominant power. History has helped to make this movement irresistible. When the Russian took refuge in Suzdal, he was compelled to clear and cultivate the very worst land of his future domain, for the black land was then overrun by nomads. How could he escape the temptation to go back and look in the South for more fertile soil, which, with less labor, would yield four times as great a harvest ? Villages and whole cantons in Muscovy have been known to empty themselves in a moment, the peasants marching in a body, as in the old times of the invasions, toward the "black soil," the "warm soil," of the South. Government and the landholders were compelled to use the most horrible means to stop these migrations of the husbandmen.

Without these repressive measures, the steppes would have been colonized two centuries earlier than they were. The report that the Czar authorized emigration, a forged ukase, a rumor, any thing was enough to uproot whole peoples from the soil. The peasant's passion for wandering explains the development of Cossack life in the plains of the South ; it explains the legislation which, from the beginning of the sixteenth century, chained the serf to the glebe and bound him to the soil. In the thirteenth century, on the other hand, the peasant was free. His prince encouraged him to emigrate, and hence came the colonization of Eastern Russia. The Russian race has the faculty of absorbing certain aboriginal stocks. The Little Russians assimilated the remnants of the Turkish tribes ; the Great Russians swallowed up the Finnish nations of the East.

The qualities of the Russian peasant fit him admirably for this great work of the absorption of other races, especially races whose civilization is of a lower type than his own. " He is good-natured, long-suffering, conciliatory, capable of bearing extreme hardships, and endowed with a marvellous power of adapting himself to circumstances." Arrogance and the assumption of personal or national superiority are wholly foreign to him. He occupies a few acres, tills his land in peace, mingles with the natives in the friendliest way, and the two races soon blend together and become one community, and finally one people.

Vámbéry says:

There has been no standstill in the Russian State from its infancy to this day. We have seen that while processes of crystallization were going on in one part of the gigantic Empire, there were already springing up new formations in other parts of it, caused by the accession of new and fresh elements. The influence of ancient Rome in revolutionizing the ethnical relations of Europe can alone be compared in a certain degree with the Russianizing influence of the Russian State on Europe, with this difference, however, that the results attending the process of transformation under Russian agencies, whilst they are not more rapid in developing than in the case of Rome, are far more intense in their effect. We have no authentic statistics at our disposal concerning the progress of population in Russia during the last century, but if we consider that there were, at the most, thirty millions of Russians at the beginning of this century, and that their number has risen within recent times up to eighty millions, it will not be difficult to guess where the Voguls, Ostyaks, Tchermisses, and other nations about whose large numbers travellers of the last century have given us information, have got to. We neither wish to, nor can we, here speak of all the particulars of the process of amalgamation ; the process remains forever the old one.

First appear on the stage the merchant and the Cossack ; they are followed by the Popa, with his superstition and worship of images, and the rear is brought up by the Vodki and the Tchinovniks with their train of Russian peculiarities, and they all manage very soon, with due regard to local circumstances, to insinuate themselves into the good graces of the natives, an achievement which seldom meets with any resistance, owing to the prevailing Asiatic characteristics of Russian society. In due course of time, the natives, continually imposed upon in their dealings with the crafty Russian merchant, fall victims of pauperism ; the holy-water sprinkle and the brandy flask inaugurate the process of denationalization, a process which is hastened by the cleverly inserted wedges of Cossack colonies, and half a century of Russian reign has proved sufficient to turn Ural-Altaians of the purest Asiatic stock into Aryan Russians. The physical characteristics alone survive for a while, like ruins of the former ethnical structure ; but even these last mementos become obliterated by the crossing of races which results from intermarriage, and we meet to-day genuine Russians in countries where in the last century no traces of them could have been found.

Wallace thus describes the changes still going on :

During my wanderings in the Northern provinces, I have found villages in every stage of Russification. In one, every thing seemed thoroughly Finnish : the inhabitants had a reddish-olive skin, very high cheek-bones, obliquely set eyes, and a peculiar costume ; none of the women and very few of the men could understand Russian, and any Russian who visited the place was regarded as a foreigner. In a second, there were already some Russian inhabitants ; the others had lost something of their pure Finnish type, many of the men had discarded the old costume and spoke Russian fluently, and a Russian visitor was no longer shunned. In a third, the Finnish type was still further weakened ; all the men spoke Russian and nearly all the women understood it ; the old male costume had entirely disappeared, and the old female costume was rapidly following it ; and intermarriage with the Russian population was no longer rare. In a fourth, intermarriage had almost completely done its work, and the old Finnish element could be detected merely in certain peculiarities of physiognomy and accent.

And Wallace, as well as Leroy-Beaulieu, remarks the

greater persistence of former race characteristics among the women than among the men.

From the continuation of this work of consolidation up to the present time, as well as from Russian history, it is evident that the Russian people is in a state of formation both moral and material. Its power is less to-day than its size or population. Its weakness in the Crimean and Bulgarian wars is an evidence of this. But this is the weakness of infancy and not of old age, and will disappear with the firmer fibre of a larger growth.

Most of the capitals of the governments in the South and East are younger than the capitals of the Atlantic States of North America. The great metropolis of Odessa is less than a century old. These new districts of Russia have increased tenfold in less than one hundred years. This is caused by colonization and the process of fusion with the native races which accompanies it. This process of fusion becomes more and more rapid as facilities for communication increase.

Sociology has shown that compound races, where the elements composing them are not too incongruous for admixture, are the best races. Indeed, the Anglo-Saxons have furnished proof of this as well as the French and the Italians. The union in these cases was accomplished centuries ago. The union of the Gauls and Franks, as well as that of the Lombards and the Latins took place before the Norman-Saxon fusion, and the vigor of these peoples has not lasted like that of the Anglo-Saxon. But this same process is going on in Russia to-day just as it is in America, where large immigration and the admixture of Celtic and German blood is improving the American stock. Russians seeem to have the faculty of absorbing greater varieties of the human species than Anglo-Saxons. No difference of race, language, or color seems to stand in their way. The very names of the aborigines become changed as soon as the heel of Russian conquest has trodden over their land. Lieutenant Alikhanoff, the adventurer who planned the capture of Merv, was the Asiatic Mussulman, Ali Khan. When he became a Russian, the addition of a suffix gave him a new name. The identity of the conquered race is lost in this great process of amalgamation. There is not an office in the Russian State, to which the most savage of its subjects is not as eligible as the native of St. Petersburg. General Melikoff, whose power was second to that of the Czar alone, was not a Russian, but a Georgian. In most places no difference is recognized in law, custom, or education. The Russian is the only language taught in the schools, official business is transacted in no other tongue. The natives who acquire it rise rapidly in the service. In Poland this transmutation has been brought about under circumstances of great cruelty. The Poles loved dearly their language, their church, their ancient institutions. Their civilization was at least equal to that of Russia. The forcible up-rooting of all that was dear to them has been a source of great sorrow and suffering.

Similar changes are accomplished by force elsewhere. Colonies of Russians are sent into new districts by Imperial command. Great numbers of men are exiled for various offences from different portions of Russia, and

compelled to live in other parts of the empire, thus keeping the whole of Russian society in a state of motion,
and preventing in great degree the fossilization which
so commonly follows upon the footsteps of autocratic
rule. The Russian people are patient and submit to
these changes without a murmur. When criminals are
exiled to Siberia, their families accompany them, and these
convict settlements form nuclei for the growth of infant
colonies. This process of colonization by force aids materially the vast currents of voluntary colonization produced by the adventurous spirit of the Russians themselves.
Even the Church, a conservative force elsewhere, encourages this growth, and the great monasteries of the Black
Clergy have often been the outposts of Russian civilization.
Add to this the fact that all emigration from Russia is
prohibited, that Russia does not recognize the right of
any of her subjects to change his allegiance or nationality,
that the Russian can never leave his province, his country,
nor his town, without the permission of his government,
which is refused if he intends permanent expatriation, and
we have a system which insures for a long time the constant growth of the Russian people. Statistics are accessible for only a short time back, but from them we learn
that the population of Russia doubles in somewhat less
than sixty years. This is slower than the growth of
the United States, which is aided by a large influx of
foreign immigrants. There is comparatively little immigration into Russia; the growth is internal. When industrial conditions change, emigration to America may
cease. But in Russia we have the assurance of a constant

increase in population. One peculiar feature in Russian social life tends to secure the rapid growth of the people by natural multiplication. The individual ownership of property in all other civilized states brings with it some restriction to the growth of population. The larger the family the less must be the share of each child in the patrimony. But in Russia, where the inhabitants of each village own its land in common, the share of each family is in proportion to the number of male members; or in proportion to the number of the heads of households. The greater the number of male children the larger will be the share of the family in the communal land, either when the child is born or when he becomes the head of a new household. The growth of population is thus encouraged, and it is natural that it should be much more rapid in Russia than in the countries of the West. The great drawback up to the present time has been on account of unfavorable conditions of climate and hygiene. Russian families are very large, but the mortality is very great. The great mass of the people have hitherto known nothing of medicine, surgery, or the laws of health. The natural increase in population has been much checked on this account. The wretched food, the long fasts prescribed by the church, drunkenness, insufficient ventilation in winter, the filthy habits of the peasantry, the contagious diseases common in the villages,—all these things make the death-rate very high. Most of these difficulties, however, can be avoided by greater knowledge and care, and there has been a decided improvement of late years. With proper precautions, the severity of the climate is no great drawback, as the high average duration of human life in Scandinavia abundantly proves. If the present communal system lasts, the birth-rate will continue to be great, while a better knowledge of the laws of health will materially lessen the mortality.

CHAPTER IV.

THE MILITARY AUTOCRACY.

IT is not only the vast area and constantly increasing population of Russia which qualifies her for that career of universal dominion to which she aspires, but also the character of her political institutions, now unique among the great powers of the world. It is the complete and absolute unity which her autocracy gives, it is the strength of her military institutions which threatens civilization. A peculiar fitness for this form of government seems now to be ingrained in the Russian people, not indeed by nature, for the Slav races were originally free, but by the force of long-continued custom. Among the great mass of the Russian people (kept ignorant indeed by this same despotism), an autocratic government is the highest ideal, and the Holy Father, the Czar, is looked upon with the deepest reverence. When, upon the accession of Anna Ivanovna, after the time of Peter the Great, it was proposed to limit her authority, many of her subjects expressed the strongest dissatisfaction, and demanded that she should remain absolute ruler, which she did. Autocracy has a useful servant in the Russian Church. The Roman hierarchy has been some-

times a source of strength, but at others a source of
weakness to monarchy. The concentration of the religious
thought of a people upon a foreign object, has often diminished their loyalty to their own sovereign. The Russian
Church is a purely national institution, and is wholly sub-
servient to the temporal power of the Czar. It was one
of the most formidable instruments in the making of the
despotism. Every dignitary in it, from the patriarch to
the curate, held his place in absolute dependence upon the
will of the Prince. The notions of autocracy came into
Russia from Byzantium, with the Church. Absolute and
unquestioned obedience to the will of the Czar is part of
the religion of every Russian, indeed the chief part. It
is impressed upon him as his highest duty by a clergy
who are the facile instruments of the Czar for that purpose. Rebellion is something beyond ordinary heresy
and sacrilege. The thoughts of the people are bound in
spiritual chains, quite as effectually as their bodies are
subject to physical power. There is as little liberty of
thought as of action; the dread of spiritual punishment is,
perhaps, more effective than the fear of Siberia or the
fortresses.

In Russia only has autocracy been able to withstand
the influences of modern civilization. Nicholas was
perhaps more an autocrat than any of his predecessors.
He regarded not only the earth, but the very skies of
Russia as his possessions. Not even in thought would he
permit his authority to be questioned. Whatever it may
do in the future, the revolutionary spirit in Russia has
as yet touched only the upper layers of society; it is

found mostly among the small class of the well educated. It destroyed a czar, it may overthrow a dynasty, but it must have a much greater growth than it has yet attained to up-root from Russia the despotic principle which has been so long ingrained in the fibre of its political organ-ism. The Anglo-Saxon form of government is still a long way off from the Russian people. Whatever consti-tution may in the future be given to Russia, it is certain that it will at first tend more than the organic law of other states to the centralization of political power. In-dividual life will still be largely regulated by government agencies. It would take some time (even if the govern-ment were so disposed) to lift a hundred million people out of the ignorance and habits of unquestioned obedi-ence to which the despotism has accustomed them.

The absence of great centres of population has also fa-vored the growth and maintenance of the despotic princi-ple; there is no point where the forces of resistance can combine. Only seventeen of all the Russian cities have a population of over fifty thousand. Not more than one tenth of the people dwell in cities. Russia is a strange example of the survival, in our own age, of a type of civilized society almost wholly militant; a nation ruled as if it were an army. Except in the tiny village commu-nities, local self-government is confined to the most trifling matters; a few bureaus at the capital direct every thing. The growth of the Russian people is by militant methods, totally different from the industrial methods of English development. The political integra-tion of Russia contrasts in a manner most menacing with

the process of disintegration which is going on everywhere in the British Empire.   In spite of the immense
industrial growth of England and her colonies, the political bonds between them are becoming weaker.   The
distant colonies, such as Canada, Australia, and South
Africa, inhabited by Anglo-Saxon peoples, are almost
wholly independent.   A certain moral support is about all
that the mother country can count upon.   They are
little better than friendly nations, the ties have been vol-
untarily relaxed in favor of local self-government and in
the interest of individual liberty.   The agitation for
home rule in Ireland leads us to think that a similar
policy will be pursued at no distant time with respect
to that island.   A great blessing is conferred upon
humanity by this policy if the Anglo-Saxon race is to
remain predominant.

A work written by H. Y. S. Cotten, of the Bengal Civil
Service, " New India, or India in Transition," demon-
strates that the present mode of governing that empire
cannot last ; that the British administration does not
respond to the currents of native thought and feeling,
that even the English ideas, absorbed by the peoples of
Hindostan, have made them less satisfied with a foreign
yoke, which is itself inconsistent with those ideas ; that
the English and the natives do not understand each
other, and there is a strong desire on the part of the
latter to govern themselves in their own way.   The English claim to have been educating them for the duties and
responsibilities of self-government, and the tendency will
be toward the granting of this at no very distant day.

Mr. Cotten insists that the future of India will be a federation of independent powers, cemented together by the power of England.

But this policy, both in India and elsewhere, so salutary in other respects, may render England all the more unable, in a military point of view, to cope with her great antagonist, whose social forces are moving in an opposite direction.   In the great struggle to come, England will be aided by the self-interest and the affection of a large number of dependent industrial peoples, averse to war, from whom she can compel little against their will.   She will be confronted by an antagonist whose nation is an army, whose citizens are accustomed by habit and inheritance of thought to obey the slightest wish of the central authority which can direct the energies of every man in the Russian dominions toward the accomplishment of a single object.

The Russian army is to-day the largest in the world. In time of war it can be augmented to more than three millions of men.   At the present moment the Russian soldiers may not be equal to their English rivals; but they possess great staying qualities.   Ever since the time of Peter the Great they have learned how to conquer through defeat.

The Russian soldier is thus described by M. Cucheval Clarigny:

Docile, as well as brave, easily contented, supporting without complaint all fatigues and privations, and ready for every thing ; the Russian soldier constructs roads, clears canals, and re-establishes the ancient aqueducts.   He makes the bricks with which he builds the forts and the barracks which he inhabits ; he fabricates his own cartridges and projectiles ; he is a mason, a metal-founder, or a carpenter, according to the need of the hour, and the day after he is dismissed he contentedly follows the plow.

With such instruments at its disposal the Russian power will never give way. A few years will suffice to render final the conquest of any land on which it has set its foot.

Another great advantage of autocracy over English liberalism in war is this: A policy dependent upon the will of one man only is pretty sure to be persisted in. It must be a very weak czar who will waver from month to month, or from year to year in his purposes, while the English government, depending for its existence upon the majority of the House of Commons, is subject not only to a change in the policy of the ministry, but to sudden changes in the ministry itself. The British constitution is defective in giving effect too quickly to sudden revolutions in popular thought. While a government ought to embody the thought of the people, it should be its permanent conviction, and not its mere temporary impulse. A ministry coming in on some fresh tide of popular passion may completely overthrow the plans of its predecessors. In war, such a system is almost as bad as the old Roman plan of dividing the leadership of an army between two generals, and providing that each should be in command a single day. In constancy of purpose do we find the key to success.

It looks now as if the conflict between England and Russia cannot much longer be postponed. Should it last long, and involve great sacrifices, the English people might think it better to give up their Asiatic possessions than to continue to defend them at too great a cost. The cry of " Perish India " is sometimes heard, and in the presence of the great social struggles which are looming up before the English people, the land question, the Irish question, the labor question, the desire of England to retain its foreign possessions is likely to grow less and less. The sceptre is passing from the land-owning and cultivated classes of England to those who have a hard struggle to earn their daily bread, who have no time to care for prestige and political power, who will not sacrifice their own interests for objects as distant as China or India. Let India fall, and Russia is assured the domination of the continent.

CHAPTER V.

WHEN we consider the probable growth of the Russian Empire in the future by the light of what it has already done, we find enough to appall the imagination. When the Russian people first appear in history, they occupy a territory considerably less than one fifth of their present European possessions alone. The former capital of Russia, Moscow, was built upon lands conquered from Asiatic races; the present capital, St. Petersburg, upon lands wrested from the Swedes as late as the time of Peter the Great. The little plateau of Valdai, in the Northwest of Russia, is the source of three great river systems, the Ilmen, connecting it with the great lakes and rivers in the North country, the Dnieper, flowing South into the Black Sea, and the Volga flowing Southeast into the Caspian. This was the cradle of the Russian people. The early capitals, Kief and Novgorod, were upon the Dnieper and the Ilmen respectively. Along these channels spread the ancient civilization of Russia; from Novgorod to the Northeast, finally reaching the shores of the White Sea and the Arctic Ocean; from Kief to the Southwest, menacing even the power of Byzantium; and later, after the

42

temporary overthrow of Kief, Russia went East to Moscow, and on to the Urals, and Southeast along the Volga to the Caspian, and across the Urals to Siberia. Then began the struggle with Sweden for the provinces upon the Baltic. Then the Cossacks of South Russia were united with the Muscovite empire, and vast tracts of land were wrested from the Turks. Then came the struggle with Poland, resulting in the three partitions of that unhappy kingdom. Then followed the seizure of Finland from the Swedish monarchy. Then the Caucasus fell, and new acquisitions were made from Persia and Turkey. Then the country of the Amoor was wrested from China and Saghalien won by shrewd diplomacy from Japan; then the network of Russian conquest enveloped the plains of Turkestan and spread to Afghanistan, while Mongolia and Thibet have been carefully explored with a view to future annexation. Colonel Prejewalsky says that during his expedition to Thibet in 1884–1885—

A portrait of the Czar acted like a charm. When it was shown to the people they went into raptures. The conviction grows in Thibet that the " Divine figure of the North will soon extend his protection to the expectant Mongols who are sick of Mandarin tyranny."

Prejewalsky further says:

The much-lauded two centuries of friendship between Russia and China, notwithstanding all our efforts to prolong it, even at the price of concession and indulgence, hang in reality by a thread which any day may snap asunder. The favorable

solution of the many vexed questions which confront us is
hardly to be attained by peaceful means. It may be that the
moment for war is not far distant. Whether we like it or not,
we have a long account which must be settled, and practical
proof given to our haughty neighbors, that Russian spirit and
Russian courage are equally potent factors, whether in the
heart of Great Russia or in the Asiatic Far East.

No geographical nor ethnographical limits have been
broad enough to confine Russian ambition. Her boundaries
are changing from year to year; no man can foresee the
end.   Let the conquered peoples speak what language
they will, let their skin be of whatever color, let their religion be what it may, Catholic as in Poland, Protestant
as in Finland, Pagan as in Siberia, Moslem as in Turkestan, it is all one; they soon become parts of the great
Russian race.   Who can draw the limits of this power of
expansion? We have evidence enough that Russian ambition has many times plotted conquests which have not
yet been made.   Catharine the Second, who divided Poland with Austria and Prussia, planned a division of the
Turkish Empire also. Paul the First held correspondence
with Napoleon, and ordered an army of invasion to set
out for India. The Moscow *Gazette* in 1832 declared that
the next treaty with England must be made at Calcutta.
Nicholas began the war which terminated in the Crimea, for
the possession of the Ottoman Empire and his proposition
to the English ambassador for a division of the sick man's
assets, can hardly have faded from the memory of many who
are still living. The last Turkish war was fomented by Russian emissaries in the Balkan peninsula for a like purpose.

There is no better illustration of the greed of Russia, and of the unprincipled manner in which she seeks to absorb her smaller and weaker neighbors, than the events which took place in Bulgaria in the year 1886. The sovereign of that country was deeply beloved by his subjects, but because, in obedience to their wishes, he was unwilling to carry out the policy of Russia at the time of the revolution in Eastern Romelia, Russia determined that he should no longer rule. First, he was dismissed in disgrace from the colonelcy of a Russian regiment to which he had been appointed. We next read that the Russian newspapers are urging the Czar to intervene in Bulgaria unless Prince Alexander is deposed by his own subjects. Bulgaria is infested with Russian agents. Bulgarian regiments are corrupted by Russian gold, and on the 20th of August a regiment of cavalry is detained in Sofia after nightfall when other troops had retired to their barracks, and about three o'clock in the morning they surround the palace of the prince. Alexander is in bed. The revolutionary leaders force their way to his ante-chamber and seize him. He is made a prisoner on his own yacht and conducted to Russia. The report is spread that he has abdicated. The Russian press now announces that it does not believe the other powers will interfere with Russia's " direct pacification of Bulgaria." Zankoff, the leader of the insurrection, is made minister, and proclaims that the Czar will protect Bulgaria. But the crime of the capture of Alexander is so infamous that the Russian government does not dare to avow openly its participation in the measure. Alexander lands at Reni, but Russia does not venture to detain him within her borders. He finds that his people have arisen almost to a man in his behalf. A great concourse meet him at every point. Soldiers who joined the insurrection confess that they received twenty rubles each, and were told that Alexander had plotted to sell Bulgaria to the Turks. DeGiers says that Russia will not occupy Bulgaria while it remains tranquil, but that Russia's position will be critical should Alexander insist upon executing the conspirators. Now, if Russia did not incite the revolt, of what interest is it to her whether or not political crime is punished in a neighboring country ? Zankoff is arrested, but Alexander is compelled to order his release. On August 30th, Alexander sends a most submissive telegram to the Czar. The Czar replies: " I cannot approve of your return to Bulgaria, foreseeing from it sinister consequences to the kingdom so sorely tried. . . . Your Highness must decide your own course; I reserve to myself to judge what my father's venerated memory, the interests of Russia, and the peace of the East, require of me."

Alexander now finds himself abandoned by the other powers. Germany, Austria, and Russia forbade him to execute the plotters against him, thus depriving him of the very essence of power. So he resigns. He says: " I cannot remain in Bulgaria, for the Czar will not permit me. I am forced to quit the throne. The independence of Bulgaria requires that I leave the country; if I did not, Russia would occupy it." Regents are appointed. The Czar agrees to recognize the regency *on condition that no*

acts of violence be committed, and acts of violence are continually incited by Russian agents. The Bulgarian Sobranje resolve to court-martial the officers inculpated in
kidnapping Alexander.

But soon the conspirators, instead of being punished,
are demanding, by means of Russian influence, a direct
representation in the government. Kaulbars is sent as
Russian agent, and thanks *Zankoff and his friends* for
their kindly welcome, asking *them* (not the regency) to
announce throughout the country that the Czar will give
protection to Bulgaria on condition *that full confidence be
placed in him.* Kaulbars declares that political prisoners
must be released and the state of siege raised, and unless
Russia's demands are obeyed he will leave Bulgaria, and
the occupation of the country will follow. He demands
the indefinite postponement of the election for members
of the National Assembly; but this is not done. He
accuses the Bulgarians of insubordination, and declares
that Russia cannot allow Bulgaria to try the kidnappers
of Alexander, nor can Alexander return. In the elections
four hundred and eighty representatives of the party of
the regency are chosen as against forty-one of all other
parties. The majorities are immense. But now Russia
declares the elections illegal and demands a postponement
of the Sobranje. The government refuses to yield. It
is reported that Kaulbars tries to win over several of the
Bulgarian garrisons to work a revolution in favor of
Russia.

The Sobranje decide to send to the Czar a deputation
to complain of the action of Kaulbars, but the Russian

consuls are ordered to refuse passports, and Kaulbars informs the government that Russia will regard the proceedings of the Sobranje as void. The Russian consul at Varna threatens to bombard the town unless the prefect permits free access of the Russo-Bulgarian partisans to the consulate, and Kaulbars informs the Bulgarian foreign minister that the Russian gun-boats there will vigorously affirm their importance if events render it necessary.

In compliance with the demands of Kaulbars, the plotters against Alexander are released. And now the Russian, Nabakoff, leads a band of Montenegrins at midnight and attacks the prefecture at Burgas, seizes the prefect, and proclaims Russian rule : but his revolt also, is soon quelled. These plotters too are tried, but Kaulbars declares the trial void. England and Austria are at last awakened and act with firmness to prevent further outrages. Lord Salisbury denounces "the midnight conspiracy, led by men debauched by foreign gold, which hunted Prince Alexander from the throne of Bulgaria and outraged the conscience and sentiment of Europe." Prudence will not permit an immediate resort to arms, so Russia will bide her time.

The present aggressions of the Czar are thus epitomized by Charles Marvin :

Russia has a frontier line across Asia five thousand miles in length, no single spot of which can be regarded as permanent. Starting from the Pacific, we find that she hankers for the northern part of Corea, regards as undetermined the boundary with Manchuria and Mongolia, regrets that she gave back Kuldja, hopes that she will some day have Kashgar, questions the Ameer's right to rule Afghan Turkestan, demands the gates of Herat, keeps open a great and growing complication with Persia about the Khorassan frontier, treats more and more every year the Shah as a dependent sovereign, discusses having some day a port in the Persian Gulf, and believes she will be the future mistress of the whole of Asia Minor.

Let us briefly review the course of the Russians in Turkestan during the past twenty years. Central Asia, while it contains large and valuable oases, adapted to stock-raising and many other forms of agriculture, has no such stores of wealth as would justify its conquest for its own sake. Possibly the Russians did not know this when they first undertook its subjection, but they have long since understood it, and the continued march of Russian conquest must have in view some object beyond the mere possession of these Central Asian districts. The expense of administering the government in these regions is considerably greater than the revenues derived from them, yet the Russians press their conquests farther and farther. Why do they do this? Their object is adequately explained by the words and acts of some of their own great military authorities.

The designs of the Emperor Paul, who projected a march upon India (which was to be stimulated by raising hopes of plunder in the minds of the wild nomads of Central Asia, who were to be invited to join him), were renewed in 1864, when the Russians first broke through the sand belt which then formed the Southern boundary of the empire, and took the rich and populous city of

Tashkend.   This city contained more than one hundred
thousand inhabitants.   It has been largely remodelled
by the Russians, is well built, and possesses a theatre,
a public library, etc., and is entirely hedged in by beautiful gardens and orchards that surround it.   When this
city was acquired by the Russians, Tchernayeff, the
leader of the expedition, writes : " The mysterious veil
which has hitherto covered the conquest of India, a conquest looked upon until now as fabulous, is beginning to
lift itself before my eyes."   In 1868, the overthrow of
Bokhara followed, but its independent government was
not entirely destroyed.   The Emir was permitted to remain upon the throne, but he became a vassal and the
blind instrument of Russian rule.   The administration of
the province was less expensive in this form than in any
other.   The conquest of Khiva followed in 1873, and here
too a kind of autonomy was preserved, but saddled with
an immense war indemnity, and totally dependent upon
Russia.   In 1876, Khokand was overthrown and bodily
incorporated.

But it was found by this time that these Eastern
khanates were not upon the most direct road to India.
The elevated and impassable barriers of the Hindoo-
Koosh stood in the way, and a passage must be found
more to the West and better suited to military operations
having their base in the Caucasus and on the shores of
the Caspian.   Meantime a great number of steamers had
been constructed, and were used in the petroleum traffic
on that inland sea.   A suitable harbor, Krasnovodsk, was
found on the Eastern shores of the Caspian, and Skobeleff,

the most brilliant of Russian generals, whose name became famous in the last Turkish war, projected an expedition against the native tribes.   A stretch of desert was overcome by means of a railway laid in the sand, over which the army was transported from the Caspian to the assault of Gök Tepe, a city which was heroically defended by the natives, the women fighting with the men.   Its capture was followed by the slaughter of thirty thousand inhabitants.   It was this same Skobeleff who said: "It will be in the end our duty to organize masses of Asiatic cavalry and to hurl them into India under the banner of blood and pillage as a vanguard, as it were, thus reviving the times of a Tamerlane."

Then Alikhanoff, an officer who had been degraded to the ranks for misconduct, was sent as an emissary to Merv, the ancient Maru, "Queen of the World."   He ingratiated himself with the Tekkes.   Soon Merv submitted to Russian dominion.   The Russians called it a voluntary submission, and said "they would send an officer to administer the government."   But instead of an officer an army went, which held the whole population as in a vice.   Along this Western road there is no natural impediment to an attack upon India.   A range of hills less than a thousand feet high, easily accessible to artillery, is all that lies between the Russians and Herat, the Gate of India.   From this, the road lies through fertile plains and easy passes to the Western limits of the British dominions.   Nor did the Russians stop at Merv.   An English commission was sent to adjust the boundaries of Afghanistan with the Russians, but the latter, without

waiting for the commission to do its work, advanced upon
Herat, in two directions, by the valley of the Murghab
to Penjdeh, and by the Hari-Rud to Pul-i-khatum. To
justify their encroachments upon the territory of the
Afghans, they set up a claim that the frontier of Afghanistan was fifty miles South of that shown by their own
maps as late as 1881, and that Penjdeh and the Zulfikar
Pass were North of the line. Penjdeh, in fact, had always
belonged to Afghanistan and paid tribute to the Ameer.

The Russian railway is already completed to a point
only a few hundred miles distant from the railway system of India, and the rapidity of communication from
Russia to the probable scene of the conflict (six days)
from the South of Russia to the centre of Asia) gives her
a great advantage in concentrating troops over England,
who must resort to a long and tedious line of communication by sea. Persia is little more than a vassal state;
Russia can count upon its support as well as upon that of
the wild tribes of Asia, when the prize of the immense
booty of India is placed before their imagination as the
reward of conquest. The prestige of Russia among
Asiatic peoples is immense. Witness the following extract from the Persian "Akhtar":

During the last thirty years a great deal has been said and
written by a large portion of the English press and influential
statesmen about the growing hostility between Great Britain
and Russia. But as yet they have done nothing, and the Russians know very well that, apart from these threats, empty out-
cries, and unsuccessful protests, they have nothing to fear
from the English. The Russians, therefore, have not heeded

in the least this flood of empty words, and have proceeded un-
disturbed and unchecked in the carrying out of their plans.
The English have always and everywhere pursued their own
interests of state, and, in our opinion, the Russians are much
more justified in the pursuit of similar objects, if we consider
their close proximity to the Mohammedan countries in question. Besides, Russia possesses greater power and authority
than England. She has a better right to undertake conquests,
because she shows a greater respect for the laws and rights of
the natives than England, who, as we have seen, is meddling
in the most shameless manner with the affairs of India, Aden,
Cyprus, Afghanistan, Egypt, Zanzibar, and Beloochistan.

Makdum Kali, a Turkoman bard, predicted not long
ago, that the whole of the world would succumb to the
power of Russia. This is the Asiatic idea of it. It is
true, the Russians have frequently declared they have no
designs on India, but in 1882 M. DeGiers said that
they had no intention of occupying Merv and Sarakhs,
both of which are to-day Russian cities. We know, moreover, that Skobeleff actually forwarded to General Kaufmann, during the last Turkish war, a plan for a campaign
in Central Asia and for exciting against England not only
Afghanistan but her own native subjects in India, and
that Kaufmann's military preparations for this purpose
had commenced, but were stopped when the Berlin
treaty was signed. What would be the conduct of the
Indian subjects of Her Majesty, in case of an invasion, is
very uncertain. English rule in India is no doubt beneficial. The people are gradually submitting to the influences of modern civilization, but this process, being

mostly voluntary, goes on much more slowly than the Russianizing of the tribes of Tartary, and is much less radical. The prejudices of the native populations are very deep-seated, nor can they wholly forget, however salutary English rule may be at present, that England was guilty of most unpardonable wrongs in the past. The English do not assimilate with them, do not intermarry, they are an alien race. Very few of them reside permanently in the country. An Englishman always looks forward to the time when he shall return. The absenteeism which has been the foundation of so much dissatisfaction in Ireland, exists also in India. The natives feel that they are being exploited for the benefit of Englishmen, and however beneficial the process may be to them, they do not like to have good done to them in this way against their will. This, together with the continually increasing vacillation of the home government from party changes and otherwise, weakens greatly the power of Great Britain to defend her Asiatic possessions.

CHAPTER VI.

THE designs of Russia upon India and Constantinople have been suspended at the present time in favor of her still more vast designs upon the Chinese empire. The possession of this empire would secure to her an undoubted supremacy, not only in Asia, but in the whole Eastern continent and in the world. If Russia can make the vast population of China a part of her military system she need fear no rival upon earth.

Let us consider in some detail the character and consequences of the Russian designs upon the Chinese empire.

What are the extent, population, and resources of that empire ?

It embraces a territory nearly three times the size of our own republic. It contains a population of nearly four hundred millions—nearly one fourth the population of the whole world.

What is the character of the land ?

In the West lie the desert plains of Mongolia, the mountains and the table land of Thibet. But the Eastern half of the empire is a territory unexcelled in fertility and resources—Manchuria to the North, and China proper in

55

the South.   Manchuria is already practically under the dominion of Russia.   It is to be traversed by Russian railroads; the seacoast is already Russian; Russian influence predominates everywhere.   It is a rich country with a fertile soil and a climate similar to that of Canada, with navigable rivers, fine forests, and valleys well adapted to the culture of wheat, barley, rice, hemp, indigo, and tobacco; a land well filled with live-stock, and containing abundant mineral resources.

China proper, with a climate like our own, is one of the most fertile regions on the globe.   The fact that it supports a population of three hundred and fifty millions is proof of this.   North of the Yellow River, the most important crops are millet and barley.   In the central and southern districts, rice and wheat thrive well; tea, cotton, sugar, oranges, bamboo, and silk are important products.   The West abounds in valuable timber.   The mineral wealth of the country is mostly undeveloped, but it is very great.   Iron ore in vast quantities is found in many places far removed from each other, indicating a wide distribution.   There is gold in many provinces, copper and lead in Southern China, and extensive salt works in the North.   The coal mines are inexhaustible. In the province of Shansi coal is sold at the mine at thirteen cents a ton.   There is more coal in that province alone than in Pennsylvania.   Tea and silk are still the largest products for foreign export.   So rich is the land and so varied the climate that there is probably no product of our own country which cannot be produced in China.

What is the character of the four hundred millions of human beings which the Chinese empire contains ?

In the Northwest we have the Mongols, descendants of Genghis Khan, who some centuries ago conquered the whole of Asia, as well as most of European Russia. In Thibet we have a race of hardy mountaineers. In Manchuria we find a people, vigorous, thrifty, intelligent, conservative, a people which has three times conquered China itself. The Manchu dynasty reigns in China to-day.

But it is with the Chinese proper, who form the bulk of the population of the Empire, that we are most concerned. "Among the various races of mankind, the Chinese is the only one which in all climates, the hottest and the coldest, is capable of great and lasting activity." "The predominant quality of the Chinaman is his industry. He has almost a passion for labor. In search of it he compasses sea and land." In addition to his power of endurance, his manual dexterity in the minutest kinds of handicraft is well known. His intellectual characteristics are peculiar, and in some respects very high. His memory is phenomenal. There are Chinamen who can repeat by heart all the thirteen classics of China. The Chinamen who come to study in our colleges are intelligent. The Chinese have untiring patience, unfailing good humor and cheerfulness under every kind of discomfort and bodily toil. They are greatly lacking in originality, in the power of initiative. They are the slaves of custom and conservatism. They will be an immense power under skilful leadership; they are helpless

without it.   The spirit of the Chinaman is essentially
commercial.   He is a tradesman.   He sells his labor and
everything he possesses for a price.   He is shrewd at a
bargain.   He can undersell his competitors.   He is economical to the last degree, although he will purchase
comforts and luxuries when he can afford them.   In commercial thriftiness he resembles the Jew.   '' His instinc-
tive habit is one of perpetual appraisement.   He thinks
in money.''   The co-operative spirit is very strong in
him.   Guilds, mutual-benefit societies, and all sorts of
associations fill an important space in the life of the
Chinese.   The price of Chinese labor is very low.   A
coolie can be employed at from six dollars to eight dollars a month.   An artisan's wages vary from ten to twenty
cents a day.   He works nine hours a day, and lives almost
entirely on rice and vegetables.   Under proper direction
the industrial capabilities of such a people will exceed
that of any other race existing in the world.   Moreover
the people of China are easily managed.   They are essentially tractable and peaceful.   Although they care nothing
for politics, the faculty of local self-government and
especially of family government is developed in a high
degree.   It is the central government at Pekin, and the
government of the viceroys and mandarins which is at
fault.   And the numerous secret societies, conspiracies,
and sometimes rebellions in China are the result of the
atrocious corruption and oppression of the central government, for which there is no other remedy.   Under a
skilful ruler the Chinese can be easily controlled.

In the late war with Japan the Chinese proved them-

selves to be poor soldiers, but they were sent against the
Japanese practically unarmed, unpaid, and badly fed,
under commanders conspicuous for cowardice.   Under
European officers they are brave and efficient.   Chinese
Gordon could lead them anywhere.   Dewey has recommended the Chinese of his fleet to full American citizenship on account of their bravery in the battle of Manila.
The willingness of Chinamen to undergo even capital
punishment as the hired substitutes of others, the constant readiness to die when the need arises, indicate that
the Chinese race has courage of a high order if properly
directed.   The men of Manchuria and Shan-Tung are
steady, docile, enduring, uncomplaining, and of splendid
physique.   The men from Hunan are dashing, courage-
ous, and loyal to their own leaders.   It is not hard to
see that under the command of efficient Europeans a
Chinese army, if well armed, well paid, and well treated,
would be an efficient fighting machine.

Perhaps the greatest defect in the Chinese character is
the lack of patriotism.   A Chinaman is deeply devoted
to his family and his national customs, but cares nothing
for the dynasty or the government.   This is indeed little
to be wondered at since the national government takes
small care of him except to tax him and to extort by
every possible kind of " squeeze " all that can be got out
of his hard-earned savings.   Indeed the lack of progress
in China is due more to the corruption of the government
than to perhaps any other cause.   The roads and means
of communication are suffered to fall into neglect.   The
transportation of food, clothing, and other products in

the inland provinces is almost impossible. Dreadful fa-
mines have occurred in China, depopulating vast regions,
while neighboring provinces had abundance of resources.
The Chinese officials levy duties and charges at various
points in transit, thus obstructing all commerce, while
very little of the revenue reaches the national treasury.
Official corruption is so universal that it passes without
remark or censure, while the integrity of the Chinese
merchants and bankers and their fidelity to contracts has
become proverbial.

It is over such a people as this, easily won by corruption, easily subdued in war, that Russia seeks to extend
the strong arm of her autocracy.

She has already accomplished much in the way of
territorial acquisition and still more in the way of political influence and domination. As early as 1858 Muravieff
obtained for Russia the Amoor province, a vast tract on
the north bank of that River. And in 1860, General
Ignatieff, by diplomacy, transferred to Russia the whole
Eastern coast of Manchuria from the Amoor River down
to the Northern boundary of Corea. In this territory the
Russian port of Vladivostock was established, the most
important port belonging to Russia on the Pacific coast
up to the present year, and the proposed terminus of the
trans-Siberian Railway when that great work was begun.

When the war broke out between China and Japan, in
1894, Russia again saw her opportunity. After the
Japanese victory in that contest, Japan proposed to annex
certain territory on the Eastern coast of China, but Russia
forbade it. Russia had reserved that conquest for her-

self, so Japan had to be content with Formosa. At the northern extremity of the Yellow Sea, commanding the gulf of Pechili, is the Liao-Tung peninsula. The gulf of Pechili is close to Pekin, and is the outlet of Pekin and Tien-Tsin, the commercial port of the capital. There are two harbors of great importance on the Liao-Tung, Port Arthur, of immense strategic value, and Talien-Wan, of perhaps equal commercial value. These ports are open all through the winter, and were coveted by Russia as furnishing her best outlet to the Pacific. Russia posed as the defender of China against Japanese encroachments, and by intrigue and corruption at Pekin she secured a dominant influence in the Chinese imperial court. Li Hung Chang is suspected of being the paid agent of Russia; the Empress Dowager is at the head of the pro-Russian faction in the government. At first Russia acquired the right to winter her fleet in Port Arthur,—that, she said, was all that she desired,—then she prevented the efforts of England to secure certain treaty ports for foreign commerce upon this part of the Chinese coast; then by means of intrigues, whose history will perhaps never be known, she secured a lease for ninety-nine years of Port Arthur and Talien-Wan, with the right to extend the Siberian Railway through Manchuria to these ports. She has now practical control of all Manchuria, and holds a predominant influence in Pekin itself. The Emperor, who had exhibited reform tendencies and a possible leaning toward the side of England and Japan, is suddenly deposed, his adherents have fled for their lives, and the Dowager empress, and the Russian faction are now in possession of all power. The Chinese soldiers in the capital are under the instruction of Russian officers—and Cossack troops in considerable numbers are already within the gates of the city for the ostensible purpose of protecting the Russian embassy.

In the proposed conquest of China the Russians have a powerful ally in France. Some years ago the French annexed Tongking, adjoining China on the South, not so much for the intrinsic value of the province as because it was the " key to China." England has Burmah to the west of Tongking, and thus adjoins the interior Southern provinces of China. But Tongking is upon the seaboard, and the purpose of the French seems to be, when the dismemberment of the Chinese empire comes, to drive a wedge between the British province and the valley of the Yang-tse-kiang, the richest part of China, and thus prevent British enterprise and British railways from entering China from that direction. After the Siberian Railroad is completed, and Russian power in the North of China is consolidated, it scarcely seems possible for England alone to resist the Russian advance. The combined armies of Russia and France in time of war can be raised to about five million soldiers. Great Britain at the present time has less than a million, including her Indian auxiliaries, and in any land contest she would be greatly overmatched, unless the Triple Alliance of Germany, Austria, and Italy should come to her aid. But Germany has been placated by Russia and allowed to take possession of Kiao-Chau Bay and the land back of it; and since Great Britain refused to join the Triple Alliance, any aid from the Powers composing it is more than doubtful. Great Britain can command the coast, but cannot penetrate far into the interior if opposed by Russia and France. England follows the seacoast and Russia follows the railroad. It is not hard to see that in such a conflict Russian domination is assured.

Nor is there any doubt as to the final purpose of Russia in the conquest of the East. As early as September, 1894, the *Novosti* suggested the partition of China. Prince Oukhtomsky, a friend of the Czar, laid stress upon " the inherent union and gradual confluence of Russia with the East. General Komaroff declared in the *Sveit* that " the East with all its countries, as China, Beloochistan, and even India, are by the will of Providence destined for the Russian people." " Aspiring in Europe to the conquest of Constantinople, in Asia they consider themselves the heirs and successors of the great World conquerors, Genghis Khan and Tamerlane." This is not merely the ambition of the Czar, but it is the natural and irresistible impulse of the whole Russian people, a policy which will continue whoever may be the occupant of the throne. " Russia obeys a law of sunward and seaward gravitation accelerated by the ambition of her statesmen and officials, and resulting in a course of development which must progress until it encounters the opposition of a nation stronger and better than herself." Russia is admirably adapted to the task of absorbing and utilizing the vast industrial and military resources of China. Her own people are of mixed blood — half-Asiatics. They have already absorbed the vast Mon-

golian population of European Russia and are absorbing
the population of Turkestan. Their political institutions
are not dissimilar,—small self-governing village communities at the foundation of the social fabric and a central
despotic authority at the apex. There is, however, this
essential difference,—that in China the central authority is weak and paralyzed; in Russia, it is practically
omnipotent. The strong government of the autocrat,
with its powerful initiative, is the one thing needed to
transform the inert masses of China into the most powerful human agency on earth. When the power of Russia
is consolidated in China, India too must give way.
Russia will become the mistress of Asia, and then Asia
will begin the conquest of Europe. There is absolutely
no possibility of resisting Russian aggression unless the
work is commenced at an early day.

And the Russian domination would not be ephemeral
and transitory.

There is one element of endurance in the Russian dream
which was wanting in those which have passed away into the
vistas of history. It does not depend on the genius of one
man, of an Alexander or a Napoleon ; nor on the politics of
one generation. Russian ambition is a permanent plant, with
its roots struck in the sentiments of over one hundred millions
of people. It requires no originality in statesmanship, but
proceeds like a cosmic movement, by its own laws, working
automatically, the particular men who seem from time to time
to be guiding it being but the accidents of the movement.
Fast or slow makes no difference in the ultimate progress.
Moreover, the Russian Empire is built territorily on more

solid foundations than any other, ancient or modern. Every addition goes to enlarge its compact mass, leaving no interstice for hostile lodgment on its flanks. Nor need we search deeply into the history of nations to learn what advantages belong to the people who fight with their back to the north wind. To parley with such a force is like parleying with a tidal wave. Only a sea-wall of· solid construction can set bounds to its inflow. (Colquhon.)

Henry M. Stanley declares in an article in the *Nineteenth Century* that even now Russia's acquisition of China is beyond England's power to prevent; that in order to resist it, she must join the Triple Alliance. However that may be to-day, it is evident that the time is coming when it will be beyond the power of any nation, or of any European combination, to resist it. The importance of the issue is well described in the words of Colquhoun, correspondent of the London *Times* in the Far East : '' The onward march of Russia cannot be stopped even by her own rulers unless it encounters a solid barrier, while the unchecked advance of that power seems certain to confer on her the mastery of the world.''

We have shown at least the danger of future Russian domination under favourable circumstances; let us next consider what would be the effect upon mankind of the supremacy of Muscovite power. Let us look into the history and the present condition of that great empire, that we may see, as nearly as possible, what the world would be if it should become subject to Russian influence.

CHAPTER VII.

THE HISTORY OF RUSSIA.

No one should open a history of Russia with the hope that he will get from it that gratification which most of the fields of modern history afford. There is less to attract our sympathy, less to inspire our enthusiasm, less fellow-feeling excited than in the struggle of the barons against John, of the Puritans against Charles, of the free cities of Italy against the imperialism of Germany, of the Dutch Republic against the bigotry of Philip. Somehow events seem to take the wrong track. As civilization grows, it appears only as a new bulwark of imperial power. As knowledge enters, it strengthens only the hand of the master and teaches him how to weave the more securely the toils which bind the slave. The development of agriculture fastens the serf to the soil; the opening of the mines adds new terrors to penal servitude; the conquest of the boundless steppes of Siberia provides a new place for horrible punishments to be inflicted upon the subject who offends. The growth of Russia has been the growth of all that we detest. The great sovereigns of Russia have been greatest in crime and outrage. We learn in these pages that human progress is not universal, that the

66

eddies which turn back are strong and deep. We read of
the overthrow of liberal institutions, the subjection of free
cities, the annihilation of enlightened communities, for
the sole reason that these became inconvenient or dangerous to arbitrary power. The chivalry, culture, and
magnanimity which elsewhere so often throw a glamour
over tyranny itself, and half reconcile us to its injustices,
even they are absent from these gloomy pages. The
naked form of force stands to-day, as of old, amid the
gloomy rocks of Caucasus, and rivets the same iron
through the Promethean breast of that free spirit that
gives to mortals the fire which comes from heaven.

Russian history has been wholly barren in all great intellectual struggles. It was a stranger to the Reforma-
tion and to the Renaissance. Russia has no traditions.
It has been a vast rural empire, a great state of peasant
communities, ruled by a despot and his army. Even its
church has little history in common with that of the rest
of Europe.

Another thing strikes us in Russian history: the people
do not appear to have made their own history as elsewhere ; they have rather submitted to influences which
they have had no hand in directing. It is a growth in-
fluenced more by external than by internal causes. The
normal development of the race has been hindered at
every step ; the invasion of the Mongols stopped it in its
youth and drove the civilization of Russia from its early
European channel. Then its Mongolian development
was stayed, and it was dragged back into the current of
European life by the giant arm of Peter the Great.

Let us review briefly the backward movement from freedom to autocracy. The first that we see of the early Slavs in history, we find them scattered in little villages, each village surrounded by its palisades and controlled by its communal village organization, the same which exists among the peasants down to the present time. This is called the *mir*. It is perhaps the most primitive form of organized social existence. Through all the changes which have taken place in higher organisms it has preserved its rudimentary character.

In the formation of the autocracy, these village organizations, too small to be in the way, too weak to be feared, were suffered to remain in their old shape, like the protozoa which exist to-day, remnants of the earliest form of organic life, while the highly developed monsters of the Saurian age have long since disappeared. The *mir*, or village community, is made up of all full-grown males in the village, who are free from paternal authority. Each village is a tiny patriarchal republic. A meeting may be convened by any member. It is held out of doors, the utmost confusion prevails, there is no chairman, everybody talks at once, the crowd listens to whom it will. Before any thing can be done it must be agreed to by all. There is no such thing as the rule of a majority. The conclusion reached, whatever it may be, must, like the verdict of a jury or the resolutions of a Quaker-meeting, embody the sense of the whole assembly. They talk and convince each other, until one side or the other gives in. When opinions cannot be reconciled, they sometimes fall to berating each other, and a sound drubbing is occasionally the means of bringing about that harmony of thought which their usages require. While the present law of the empire permits a majority to control, the peasants do not follow any such plan, but adhere firmly to their ancient custom. In their discussions there is the fullest liberty of speech. Even political questions are sometimes talked over by the peasants in their meetings, a thing which occurs nowhere else in Russia, and instances are known where the Starosta, their chief functionary, in the simplicity of his heart has read revolutionary proclamations which were fully considered, in utter ignorance that this was one of the highest crimes known to Russian law. These village communities are remarkable for the humanity of many of their rural customs, the duty to help those unable to work, and other fraternal notions. The highest respect prevails for the decisions of the *mir*, which are absolute and final in all matters regulating their internal affairs. The Russian proverb is, " Whatever the *mir* decides, is ordained of God."

Among the primitive Slavs there was no national union. They had little idea even of the unity of tribe. Such was their love of liberty that each village resisted all authority outside of itself. Of course no people could long exist with so little cohesive power. The Slavs were torn by dissensions. As they were unwilling to be ruled by any among themselves, a family of foreign princes was called upon to administer the government. These men (the Variagi, as they were termed) were probably of Scandinavian origin. The family of Rurik was the one from which the rulers were taken. At this time the larger

towns, which afterwards became the capitals of the principalities, were controlled in a manner quite similar to the ·
villages. The whole male population, rich and poor, were
summoned at the call of any member. This assembly
was called the *vetché*. When the princes of the House
of Rurik came, they did not change this primitive form of
organization ; they simply added to it an element of military power. The prince was accompanied by his *drujina*,
or military household of fellow adventurers, who ate at
his table and were his companions in battle. In many
of the larger towns, the authority of the *vetché* was
still practically paramount. The prince generally found
it to his interest to rule in conformity to the will of
the public assembly. In the House of Rurik, the eldest
of the blood, whether son, brother, uncle, or other relative, was chosen prince of the chief town ; but this rule
was by no means inflexible. When the prince proved
distasteful, the *vetché* assembled, and with the words
" We salute thee, O Prince," " they showed him the way
out," and he left with his *drujina* and sought another
city, while the *vetché* which had expelled him called
another prince of the house more to their taste. When a
prince died, the territory over which he had exercised this
very limited sort of dominion was generally divided
among a number of his relatives. As the princes grew in
number, the communities over which they were called to
rule also increased, until there grew up a sort of law of
political supply and demand. The best cities got the
best princes. The princes who were not satisfactory to
the larger towns were compelled to hunt up smaller com-

munities that would take them for rulers. In some of the largest cities, before the prince could exercise any authority, he was required to enter into the *riada*, or written compact, which clearly set forth the rights of the people. This was the case at Novgorod and Pskov. In Kiev, the ancient capital of Russia, as well as in many smaller towns, his prerogatives were probably greater, and the influence of the *vetché* less. If no available prince of the House of Rurik could be found, the *vetché* sometimes selected other persons, and once a simple *boyar* or noble of Russian blood was called upon to administer the government.

It is easy to see that where the continuation of the prince's authority depended upon his performing his duties in a manner satisfactory to all the people, his government would be a popular one. Even his *drujina*, his fellow adventurers, were liable to desert him if his fortunes fell.

Rurik himself was called to Novgorod as its first prince. This ancient city was built upon both banks of the Volkow, a navigable stream communicating with the great lakes and with the rivers of the North. It became at an early day a commercial centre, and was the largest and wealthiest city of Russia, containing at times a population of more than a hundred thousand souls. The whole body of the citizens was convoked at the sound of the great bell, and met in the court of Iaroslaf; any citizen, the very humblest, could call them together. The *vetché* could annul the decree of the prince, or dismiss his officers. The meanest citizen might prefer a

charge against him. It not infrequently occurred that
princes were discharged and recalled several times in succession. The republic called itself "My Lord Novgorod
the Great," and the people said: "Who can equal God
and the Great Novgorod?" The prince made an oath to
depose no magistrate without trial, and to observe the
laws and privileges of the city. He could not execute
justice without the help of the *posadnik*, the local judge,
nor take any suit beyond the jurisdiction of Novgorod.
The determinations of the *vetché*, like those of the *mir*,
were made, not by the majority, but by the unanimity of
voices.

This principle seems to be inherent in the Slav peoples. In Poland it required the unanimous choice of
the nobles to elect a king. The opposition of a single
voice could defeat the most important measures. This
led to anarchy and to the overthrow of the Polish kingdom. In ancient Novgorod, too, great trouble came from
this strange custom. Rival assemblies organized and
fought out their battles on the bridge ; a minority which
would not yield was sometimes drowned in the Volkow.
When Novgorod established colonies, each had its own
vetché for the management of its local affairs, but it was
subject to the decrees of the *vetché* of Novgorod. When
the public assembly of the parent city was to be convoked upon matters affecting one of the colonies, the
colony was notified and invited to attend, but there was
no representative government ; those who came simply
formed a part of the *vetché* of Novgorod. Such a crude
form of government could not last. When the interest of

the colony and the parent state conflicted, the colony would declare its independence. Perhaps Novgorod would accede to this; generally there was a war, but the colonies were distant and their subjugation was difficult. So it came to pass that as the colonies multiplied the process of disintegration kept going on. Pskov was originally a Novgorodian colony which became independent at an early day. Viatka was another.

When Rurik was called to Novgorod, other Variag princes, though not of the same family, were called to Kiev, a city on the Dnieper communicating directly with the Black Sea. From thence they made an expedition against Byzantium, the first of a series of similar incursions, through which Greek civilization was brought into Russia. The expedition was unsuccessful. Oleg, the brother of Rurik, conquered Kiev, and he too sailed against Byzantium, and received contributions from the Emperor as the price of peace. His successor, Igor, in a third expedition ravaged the Greek provinces. Vladimir, searching for the best religion, adopted that of the Greek church and forced baptism upon his unwilling subjects. Vladimir divided the cities of Russia among his heirs, but one of them, Iaroslaf the Great, subdued the others and assumed supreme control. His code of laws is still extant. It resembles the contemporary laws of other European nations; it permits private revenge and blood atonement, provides for trial by jury, by ordeal, and by compurgation. Torture and capital punishment were unknown. Iaroslaf held correspondence with European states. Inter-marriages were made between the House of

Rurik and other royal families. Russia of the eleventh century was a European state; it afterwards became Asiatic. Iaroslaf made of Kiev a great capital, containing four hundred churches and many schools. He was a Russian Charlemagne. He divided his principality into fiefs among his relatives and companions, but these grants were always temporary and revocable at his will.

The Variagi were called into Russia for the purpose of putting an end to the ceaseless strife of town against town. The continual partition of territory among the princes of the House of Rurik, their turmoils and dissensions after the death of Iaroslaf the Great, brought about calamities almost as great as the anarchy of the original Slavs. The only unity was that of race, language, religion, and historical development. The eldest of the house was nominally head, but had little power over the others. Gradually the tide of Russian emigration flowed East, the princes of Suzdal acquired power and attacked Novgorod. That great city became for a time subject to a prince of Suzdal named Andrei, an unflinching tyrant, and upon his assassination disorders followed everywhere. There was pressing need of greater national unity.

Suddenly, from the solitudes of the East, there came a strange and unknown power, which was to accomplish this work. In frightful suffering and bloodshed were laid the foundations of a gloomy despotism. In Eastern Asia, at the foot of the Altai mountains, lived the wild race of Tartars. Under Genghis Khan, the tribes of this nomadic people were united. China was laid waste. All in their way became a prey to these savages, who knew no distinction of age or sex. Soon these herds of innumerable horsemen swept Westward under Batui, the lieutenant of the Khan. They invaded the plains of Russia and defeated the army of Kiev at the great battle of Kalka. Then they vanished as suddenly as they had come. New conquests called them elsewhere. In a few years they returned. There was no union anywhere to resist them. Such was the discord among the princes, that one faction would invoke their aid for the destruction of another. Everywhere they went, they demanded the tribute of a tenth as the condition of peace. Terrible accounts are given of the appearance of this savage people. The whole race was an army and marched together. Their wild visages, their screams, the neighing of the horses, the bellowings of the cattle, struck terror at their approach. One after another, the cities of Russia fell before them until nothing was left but Novgorod and a small tract in the Northwest. Alexander Nevski reigned in that city. He is one of the few heroes of history whose patriotic efforts gleam brightly through the gloom of a falling cause. His bravery and intelligence were shown in his successful wars against the Livonians, Swedes, and Finns, but when this countless swarm of barbarians appeared, he saw that resistance was ruin and he advised submission. The whole of Russia bowed under the Mongol yoke.

The Tartars did not introduce any fundamental political changes. They collected the tribute of a tenth, and the Russian princes were forced to visit the Horde in token of submission. The Tartars built the city of Sarai on the lower Volga. Thither the princes went, and the lieuten-

ant of the Khan judged their disputes. Often they were
required to repair to the tents of the Great Khan himself,
at the Eastern extremity of Asia, across pitiless deserts, where their nobles and they themselves perished
from thirst, and their dry bones whitened the steppes.
The Russians were compelled to furnish troops who served
the Khan in his wars and who shared with his own soldiers the booty of his conquests. No prince could ascend
the throne or make war without the authority of the Khan.
There were inter-marriages between the Tartars and the
princes and nobles of Russia, but this amalgamation did
not extend to the lower strata of society. The peasants,
who preserved their purer blood and faith, became distinct-
ively known as Krestianin or Christians. Gradually the
Tartars became more civilized. A sort of rude chivalry
began to prevail among them, while the Russians, de-
based by their thraldom, vied with each other at the
court of the Khan in servility and intrigue. Each prince
sought to excite the Tartars against his brothers, in order
to acquire their possessions. Their sycophancy reached
the lowest depths. Gradually the principalities of Eastern
Russia grouped themselves around Moscow. A race of
princes, stern, crafty and pitiless, servile to the Khan,
arrogant to their subjects, assumed the title of Grand
Princes of Moscow, and laid the foundation of the present
autocracy. They became collectors of the Khan's tribute.
The Tartar knew no pity in his exactions and they knew
none. They ruled with merciless severity. The great
historian of Russia, Karamsin, says: "The princes of
Moscow took the humble title of servants of the Khans,

and it was by this means that they became powerful
monarchs." Rambaud says : " It was the crushing weight
of Tartar domination that stifled the germs of political
liberty." The Eastern type of government has always
been the absolute type, and both from Asia and from
Byzantium came the infusion of absolutism into the government of Russia. The Mongol yoke did not interfere
with the growth of the Greek church. This church has
been the constant ally of despotism. It planted autocratic
ideas into Russia at an early day. The arbitrary codes of
the Greek emperors, Basil and Justinian, introduced with
the new faith, were established side by side with the free
code of Iaroslaf, and the liberty-loving Slavs became
accustomed to ideas of autocracy, imprisonment, forced
labor, flogging, torture, and the death penalty. The
Tartars indeed granted special favors to the Greek church
and exempted its priests from taxation. Convents multiplied, superstition increased, while scholars and learning
disappeared.

One cannot read without sickening, the stories of the
murders, the tortures, the massacres, the intrigues, the
slavish subserviency, and the cowardly assassinations
that mark the growth of the Grand Principality of Moscow. Women and children are impaled alive, men are
burned in iron cages, excruciating tortures are prescribed
by law, mutilation of face and limb are the most ordinary
kinds of punishment. Neither ties of friendship nor of
kinship are any protection. The murder of Mikhail by
Iuri is avenged before the eyes of the Khan himself by
the son of the murdered man, Dmitri of the Terrible

Eyes. It was in the blood of many martyrs that the Holy Empire of Russia came to its growth. Great strides are made toward consolidation of power. When a prince dies, his property is no longer divided among his sons or brothers, but the paramount authority is given to one alone. Gradually the power of the Tartars becomes weakened by wars among themselves, while Russia grows stronger by the union of all authority in the hands of a single prince. Finally the Russians attempt to throw off the yoke of the Khan. Their prince defeats the Tartars in a great battle. Then Tamerlane, the conqueror of India, becomes Khan, the tide of victory ebbs, and Moscow is sacked by his lieutenant. But the Muscovites soon recover from the disaster. The principality grows in power, and the Grand Prince of Moscow becomes the ruler of Novgorod also. Tartar suzerainty is again established, and the Russian princes rival each other in baseness. The Khan confirms the right of a usurper against the lawful prince, because, bowed in the dust, he claimed "no other title to the principality but the will of the Khan himself."

At this time Byzantium fell before the conquering Turks; there was no longer a great Czar in the East. The Princes of Moscow were soon to shake off the Tartar yoke, and to assume the title.

The re-conquest of Russia from the nomads of the South had begun. The Tartars of the steppe conquered, but could not assimilate the Russians of the forest. A temporary suzerainty was all that they could maintain over a people whose agricultural pursuits and modes of life were so different from their own. The re-conquest was a task more thoroughly done. The Russian, in his turn, overcame and then assimilated. He threw off the yoke of the khans, and then, emerging from his forests of the North, to which he had been driven, he not only regained the ground he had lost, but spread the network of permanent colonization far to the South and East of his former boundaries, absorbing into the mass of the Russian people whatever of the Tartar element remained.

The Tartar population in a few cities, such as Kazan and Astrakhan, with small and scattered Tartar communities, distributed here and there like little islets in the great ocean of Russian civilization, are the only independent relics which to-day remain to attest the supremacy of these wild nomads five centuries ago. The infusion of Tartar blood into that of the Russian people has not been great, but the Tartar domination has left a lasting impress upon Russian character. It is to them that we must ultimately trace the habits of servitude and baseness, the notions of autocracy, and the craft, the dishonesty, and dissimulation, which have left their mark upon the character of the Russian people.

The consolidation of national power is generally accomplished under the leadership of some great man; that of Russia was brought about through the able and crafty policy of Ivan the Great. His reign took place during an age when, throughout all Europe, the disintegrated forces of feudalism were supplanted by the concentrated power of monarchy. It was the time when Ferdinand and Isabella had consolidated under a single throne the petty governments of Spain. It was the period when the

Tudors of England had put an end to the interminable Wars of the Roses, and had asserted an authority paramount to that of the nobles or the parliament of the people. It was the age when Louis XI., by his genius and merciless craft, had stamped out the power of feudalism and given to France a strong but absolute government. Ivan the Great closely resembled the latter monarch. He was the most devout of sovereigns; his hypocrisy knew no bounds. While he cut off the noses and lips of his prisoners, while he mutilated by horrible tortures the highest of his nobility, while he assassinated his own kindred for the purpose of appropriating the principalities which belonged to them, he kept with the utmost punctiliousness all the observances of the Church, and prayed and wept with unction for his victims. He stirred up dissensions in Novgorod which led to its final subjection. The *vetché* was wholly overthrown, and the great bell which called the people together was taken away. In his wars with Lithuania, Western Russia, which had melted away before the time of the Tartars, was partly reconquered. Ivan married Sophia Paleologus, the last descendant of the Greek emperors. Greek immigrants flocked to Moscow, bringing with them Greek letters, Greek arts, and Greek subserviency to despotism. Ivan was a law-maker, too, and the code of the Ulogenia increasing corporal punishment, the death penalty, and torture, was established during his reign.

It was said that this great tyrant was personally a coward; that his victories were won by his generals while he remained immured in his palace. The Tartars, torn with internal dissensions, troubled him but little. Under his reign their yoke was shaken off, but the Tartar domination was no more grinding than the despotism which he established. "To a Russian who said that autocracy had lifted Russia, when crushed by the Tartars, a foreigner answered that it had been lifted only upon its knees." By the Muscovite forms of servility the proudest *boyars* declared themselves slaves of the Czar. The most debasing ceremonial, descending from class to class, down to the lowest, was ennobled by the commands of religion. And yet, without the tyranny established by the Grand Princes of Moscow, Russia would never have been the great empire it is. In this period, which Solovief calls the prolongation of the liquid state, no other form of governmental organism could have created a stable empire upon these boundless plains. Solovief says that "the excessive energy of the government was a natural consequence of the weakness and incomplete development of the social body."

Vasili, grandson of Ivan the Great, suppressed the liberties of the last of the free cities, Pskov, whose weeping citizens were deprived of their *vetché* and their bell. The nobles of the city were banished, and their places were filled by three hundred Muscovite families sent to Pskov for that purpose. The annalist cries: "An eagle, a many-winged eagle, with claws like a lion, has swept down upon me ; he has taken captive the three cedars of Lebanon, my beauty, my riches, my children. Our land is a desert, our city ruined, our commerce destroyed.

My brothers have been carried away to a place where our fathers never dwelt."

All the appanages, or portions carved out for younger sons by the princes, were now destroyed; all power was united in one prince. The prince's jester rode through the streets of Moscow with a broom, crying out that it was time to clean the empire of what remained of this rubbish.

Then came Ivan the Terrible. In his time, the struggle was not against the neighboring princes, but against the oligarchy of the boyars. During his childhood, this ambitious nobility had assumed full control. Ivan was a boy who said little but thought a great deal. At last he summoned his boyars and reproached them for their evil government. "There were among them," he said, "many guilty ones, but this time he would content himself with making one example." He ordered his guards to seize Shuiski, the chief of the nobles, and then and there had him torn to pieces by hounds. Others were banished. The prince who did this was *thirteen years of age.* A period of internal peace and external conquest follows. First Kazan, then Astrakhan, strongholds of the Tartars on the Volga, fall before him. Later the intrigues of the nobles are renewed. Ivan falls dangerously ill, the boyars refuse allegiance to his son, and a mutiny breaks out in the palace. He knows the fate in store for his wife and children if he should die, but he recovers. His wife is poisoned; Kurbski, one of the most trusted of his nobles, deserts to the king of Poland; other plots are discovered. All the passions of his malignant nature become aroused. Then follow the seven periods of massacre; a reign of terror hangs over the nobles. Ivan writes to the monastery of St. Cyril, asking the prayers of the Church for his victims. The list shows thirty-five hundred; many of the names are followed by the gloomy addition, "with his wife and children," "with his sons," "with ten men who came to his help." Ivan slew his own child in an altercation. When the spirit of liberty revived in Novgorod, the revolt of that great city was punished by the physical extermination of its inhabitants. For five weeks the work of slaughter went on within its walls, and sixty thousand is the tale of men butchered by his merciless soldiery. Yet Russia grew in power under his government. In his reign, an army went across the Urals under a brigand chief, and conquered much of Siberia, " the great realm that slopes to the Arctic, that sluggish mere and motionless, where you hear the sound of the sun rising." Although Ivan was willing to use the Church as an instrument of his despotism, he was statesman enough to perceive that there was a menace in the great power of the monasteries, so he forbade them to acquire new lands. His latter years were clouded by military disasters in the West, and by the failure of his intrigues for the Polish crown.

Such was the fear of assassination at this time, that it was the custom for the relatives of the Czar's wife, and not his own, to take control of the affairs of state. Since they would be the greatest losers by his death, their efforts were directed towards the perpetuation of his life

and power. The penal code was savage. The insolvent
debtor was tied up half-naked in a public place, beaten
three hours a day for forty days, and then sold into slav-
ery. Men were broken on the wheel, impaled, drowned
under the ice, knouted to death, buried alive up to the
neck, torn to pieces by iron hooks. The noble killed his
slave and suffered no penalty. Foreigners were secluded
and rigidly watched. Even ambassadors were not allowed
to hold converse with the people, lest Russian manners
should be contaminated by the outside world. No citizen could quit the town in which he lived. The very
peasants hid their property to escape taxation. Women
dwelt in Oriental seclusion; they were always minors in
the eye of the law. They might be beaten by their hus-
bands at will. Cards and dancing were forbidden, but
drunkenness was universal. Bear-fights and the jests of
buffoons were the diversions of the people. Medical
science was unknown; medicine and sorcery were synony-
mous. If the doctor did not cure, he was punished as a ma-
gician. Society sank to the lowest depths to which thraldom can degrade it. Yet Ivan himself was not wholly a
barbarian. He was a man of no mean literary ability. He
encouraged printing and letters; but among such a people
these could make little headway.

The successor of Ivan, his son Feodor, was utterly un-
like his father. He was a good man, but a vacillating
and imbecile ruler, and the power passed to Boris Godunof, a powerful noble, who ruled with vigor in the
Czar's name. Boris prohibited the serfs from changing
their masters, and thus bound them to the soil. He insti-

tuted the patriarchate, in order to have a strong ecclesiastical support for his own claims to the throne when Feodor should die. Dmitri, another son of Ivan the Terrible and heir to the throne, is slain, presumably by the secret order of Boris, though others were punished for it. Feodor dies; the dynasty is now extinct. The patriarch supports the claims of Boris to the throne, and a sort of States-General is convened, which elects him. Suddenly a man appears claiming to be the murdered Dmitri. He invades Russia at the head of a little army of Poles and Cossacks. After several battles fought with varying success, the nobles, weary of the tyranny of Boris, desert to the standard of the usurper. Boris dies, and Dmitri enters Moscow and assumes the government. The widow of Ivan the Terrible recognizes the usurper as her son, and during his short reign of less than a year he displays many high qualities. But, upon his marriage with a Polish princess, a Catholic, the religious and national prejudices of the Russians are aroused and he falls a victim to a conspiracy among the nobles, headed by Vasili Shuiski, who succeeds to the throne upon his death. Then another Dmitri appears, a man low-born, brutal, and ignorant, and while these two contend for the sovereignty of the empire, Sigismund of Poland enters Russia at the head of an army, and his son Vladislas becomes Czar. The wildest confusion prevails between contending factions, until another States-General settles the succession upon Michael Romanoff, the first of the present reigning house. The power of autocracy is now permanently established.

Farther South, on the untilled steppes, and forming a military barrier between Muscovy and the hordes of plundering and slave-dealing Turks and Crimean Tartars, lived the Cossack tribes in a sort of wild liberty, begotten by their nomadic life. Some of these dwelt in the Ukraine, the most fertile and beautiful of the plains of Russia, whose deep black soil had not yet been invaded by the implements of systematic agriculture, since a pastoral people will not resort to the hard life of the farmer while there is land enough to support them and their flocks in comfort in their nomad state. These Cossacks formed little military republics, protecting themselves as best they might from the marauding Moslems in the South, whose territories they often invaded, bringing back with their plunder the wives of the Tartars, whose blood became thus intermingled with their own. In their social institutions the most absolute equality prevailed. In their often-recurring elections the humblest might become chief of the tribe or the nation. "Be still, Cossack, thou mayest sometime be hetman," was the answer to many a complaint. The Cossacks of the Ukraine had hitherto preserved this freedom under Polish suzerainty; a half-barbarous tribe farther South, the Zaporoshtsui, enjoyed still greater liberty, but under Alexis, the successor of Michael, they both became subject to the Czar, who granted them, for a while, a sort of semi-independence. But the Czar's power is too strong; the Cossacks resist ; they are overthrown, and their liberty is taken away.

We have thus followed the gradual withdrawal of freedom from the communities of the early Slavs, until we find the race subject to the sternest and most relentless despotism on earth.

Autocracy, now firmly established, is following the path which despotism is almost sure to take at one time or another. Russia is becoming fossilized. The influence of the Church, which has done so much to consolidate the power of the Czar, is opposed to all innovation. The minutest habits of social life are regulated by the joint authority of a Church and a State which regards every breach of its commands as a matter both of sacrilege and treason. Sunk in semi-barbarism, isolated from the rest of Europe, the Russians refuse all instruction, oppose all civilization, and believe their way the only true way, their ideals the only true ideals. He who proposes an innovation is not only a traitor to the Czar, but a rebel to the commands of the Most High.

Suddenly there sprang upon the scene of action a colossal figure—one of the few men able to break the thraldom which custom and superstition impose, to overcome the prejudices of his time; to gather for himself the stores of modern civilization, and to scatter them among his people. It was an extraordinary circumstance that such a man, by the accident of birth, held in his single hand the destiny of the whole Russian State. Without him, the reforms with which he filled a lifetime would have required centuries for their accomplishment. He was one of the few great men of history to whom the power was given to turn with his single arm the whole current of a nation's life. He tore Russia by main force

from her ancient moorings, and sent her forward upon
the swift stream of modern civilization. Peter the Great
was born a barbarian; he passed much of his turbu-
lent youth upon the streets of Moscow, associating with
everybody, acquiring knowledge from every source. To
his last day he preserved the eager curiosity of childhood,
an unquenchable thirst for information, violent passions,
but an earnest purpose, never to be shaken, of making
Russia a great state and the Russian people a great and
civilized people. Throwing aside all pomp and pageantry,
he went everywhere *incognito.* He was disguised as a
subordinate in the embassy which he sent to visit the
nations of Europe. He learned navigation from a skipper
on the White Sea, and ship-building in the garb of a work-
man at Saardam and Amsterdam. Russia should know
these things; nobody else could teach her, so he must
learn himself. Yet he was as great an autocrat as any of
his predecessors. He crushed out liberty as relentlessly
as Ivan the Great.

His great aim was to make Russia one of the great civilized states of Europe. To do this, the country must have
an outlet on the sea. It must have some commerce with
the outside world, he must own the Baltic provinces, and
to get these he must fight with Sweden. But the Swedes
are civilized, they know the modern methods of warfare,
the Russians do not. In the first encounter, the Russians
are shamefully defeated, but they can wait. Peter must
learn from his enemies. At last he is able to beat them
when fighting two to one. This is a great gain. Charles
XII. of Sweden, is a man who would play the rôle of

Alexander, but Peter says, "he will find me no Darius."
Charles invades Russia, Peter offers terms, but the Swedish
king will treat only at Moscow. The Russians retire be
fore him and draw him into the midst of their forests and
plains in the depths of a Russian winter. Hunger and
cold destroy half the army of Sweden before it encounters the Russians. Then comes Poltava, and the army of
Charles is annihilated. The star of Sweden wanes, and
Russia, with its larger resources and greater power of expansion, takes the rank which its rival held. So Peter ac-
quires his outlet on the Baltic.

It is impossible for us to imagine the difficulties which
the Czar had to overcome in forcing his reforms upon
Russia. His efforts to make the nobles shave their beards
provoked more animosity than all the massacres of Ivan
the Terrible. The old Russian proverb is "Novelty brings
calamity"; reform had to be enforced by the knout, by
banishment, by death itself. He pushed his reforms indiscriminately in every direction. In all things except
its absolute form of government, Russia must become
like its neighbors.

The Church had accomplished what it could in welding
the despotism, it now stood in the way of reform. It was
conservative of old customs, hence he limited its authority.
The patriarchate was abolished. Peter's despotism was
to be military, not monastic, his autocracy was of the kind
that crushed equally the boyar and the priest. Every
noble was required to serve the State for life. To enable
him to perform this duty, his power over his serfs must
be maintained and increased. Russia was to be a State

centralized and civilized like the France of Louis the Fourteenth, yet the patriarchal and Asiatic principle which presided over the relations of the father with his children, of the Czar with his subjects, of the proprietor with his serfs, was to remain unimpaired. On the basis of a social organization which seemed to date from the eleventh century were to be constructed a system of diplomacy, a regular army, a complete order of administrative officers, together with schools and academies, and the trade and manufactures of a luxurious civilization.

The reforms which Peter introduced have lasted down to the present time, in spite of the repugnance of the people, and the imbecility and vices of many of his successors. But the rough haste with which he forced them upon Russia did great harm. He took no note of moral laws ; he weakened the conscience of his people by violating it. By copying every thing from other sources, he gave no play to Russian originality. Had he paid some heed to the law of natural selection, his reforms might indeed have come slower, but he would have planted in Russia only such things as were capable of growth on Russian soil. As it was, he brought into Russia institutions which were not in accord with the spirit of the people, and which, like borrowed garments, would not fit. So long as serfdom, with its primitive and patriarchal customs, continued to exist, civilized institutions, affecting only the upper strata of Russian society, were grotesquely inharmonious. This dualism of Russian civilization is to-day repeated in Russian character. The most opposite extremes are found together.

To a large extent, the old nobility was supplanted by the so-called nobility of merit, the nobility of office-holders, the various gradations of the Tchin, established by Peter, where appointments and promotion depended upon service to the State. Peter decreed that land should go to the oldest by birth. · The seclusion of women was abolished, for this was opposed to the civilization of Europe, and was not necessary to the support of his power. Women were no longer compelled to marry against their will. The corruptions of office-holders had been frightful. Men solicited offices of the Czar that they "might feed themselves" by plundering the people; these things were mercilessly punished. A State Inquisition was established for "crimes against the majesty of the Czar." Peter's method of enforcing his reforms strikes us with wonder at its barbarous simplicity. All towns must send shoemakers to learn the trade at Moscow; beards were taxed; no Russian must become a monk until thirty years of age, lest population be diminished. He determined to establish a new capital by the sea; he would tear the Russians away from their old associations around Moscow. St. Petersburg was built by edicts; he decreed that there should be no stone house erected except at the new capital; all stone-masons flocked thither at once. Every owner of five hundred peasants must build a house in that city. The capital of Russia remains a durable monument to his energy. His motto contained the secret, not only of his own greatness, but of the continued greatness of the Russian State, " *Vires acquirit eundo.*" The continued movement of Russian society has pre-

served it from the crystallization into which it was falling
when he took the helm.

Peter the Great was, perhaps, more than any other
sovereign in history, a type of the people whom he ruled.
In the words of Leroy-Beaulieu :

This union, in a single person, of so many qualities and
defects, of so many traits scattered through a nation, formed
a man, wild, strange, almost a monster, but at the same time
one of the most vigorous and enterprising men, one of the best
endowed for life and action which the world has ever seen.
Few nations have the good-fortune of thus having a great man,
in whom they can themselves be personified, who, even in his
vices, seems a colossal incarnation of their genius.   Peter, the
pupil and imitator of foreigners ; Peter, who seemed to have
made it his mission to do violence to the nature of his people,
and who was looked upon by the old Muscovites as a sort of
Anti-Christ, is the type of the Russian, the Great-Russian in
particular.   With him it can be said that the sovereign and
the nation explain each other.   A people who are like such a
man are sure of a great future ; if they seem to lack some of
the highest and finest qualities which adorn humanity, they
possess those which confer power and political greatness.

Under the reign of Elizabeth, the daughter of Peter,
while religious persecution increased, the death penalty
was abolished, but a hundred blows of the knout (which
the victim rarely survived) followed by lifelong exile to
Siberia, with nose and ears cut off, was an indifferent
substitute.   Eighty thousand prisoners were knouted and
banished during her reign.

Foremost among the successors of Peter was Catharine the Second.   Her skilful intrigues in Poland, her defeat of the Turks, her conquests in the South, and the extension of the territory of Russia in every direction under her administration, present a brilliant chapter in Russian history.   But it is with her internal policy that we are most concerned.   At the beginning of her reign her ideas were extremely liberal; she established a commission to compile a new code, and gave to the commissioners instructions as to the principles which should govern them, taken from the brightest pages of the philosophy of the 18th century.   It contained such maxims as the following: "The nation is not made for the sovereign, but the sovereign for the nation."   "Equality consists in the obedience of the citizen to the law alone; liberty is the right to do every thing that is not forbidden by law."   "It is better to spare ten guilty men than to put one innocent man to death."   "Torture is an admirable means for convicting an innocent but weakly man, and for saving a stout fellow even when he is guilty."

She talked of the emancipation of the serfs; she established a society which proposed the question of emancipation as a subject for prize competition.   An article favoring it won the prize.   But Catharine did nothing more.   Indeed, she finally aggravated serfdom by dividing many of her own serfs among the nobles.   She forbade peasants to complain of their masters.   A master might send his serf to Siberia at will.   She allowed no courts for determining the rights of serfs belonging to nobles.   She followed the policy of Peter in limiting the power of the

Church; she protected religious refugees from other countries; she appropriated a vast part of the domains of the monasteries; she granted religious toleration. It would appear from her correspondence with Voltaire that she was personally a skeptic. She introduced a number of superficial reforms among the upper classes; she took measures for the instruction of women, encouraged education, and established a hospital for foundlings at Moscow; but her reforms went no deeper than the upper classes of Russian social life; the serfs were more abased than ever. When the French Revolution shook the thrones of Europe, a great change took place in Catharine's ideas. She had the bust of her old friend, Voltaire, removed to the rubbish-room. Russians suspected of liberal ideas were closely watched; the author of a book on serfdom, containing views similar to those which she had held herself, was sent to Siberia. Several public journals were suppressed; she broke off all communication with France, forbade the tricolor to enter Russian ports, and expelled French subjects who would not swear fidelity to monarchy. Despotism received new strength at the hands of this brilliant but unprincipled woman.

Her son Paul, brought up by Catharine in seclusion from motives of jealousy, was a tyrant by nature. Under his reign the censorship of the press became more rigorous. Foreign travel was forbidden.

Paul was succeeded by Alexander, whose international policy, disastrous at first, ended in the overthrow of Napoleon, and made him the chief among the allied monarchs of Europe. An advent of liberalism came in with his reign, the censorship was mitigated, and travel encouraged. Even a constitution was talked of; the emancipation of the serfs was projected; contracts of manumission were made valid; dissenters were tolerated; public education was organized. Under the advice of Speranski, elaborate schemes were prepared for the reform of the State; but at last those interested in the support of existing institutions became leagued against him, and Speranski was overthrown. He was succeeded by the reactionary Araktcheef. Then Alexander's own character seemed to change; he became more and more conservative. The press was again subjected to the strictest censure. We find that even the works of Grotius on International Law, as well as the theories of Copernicus, were interdicted. The Czar grew gloomy and suspicious, and considered himself the dupe of his own sentiments. The system of military colonies, which has since been used with such wonderful effect, was commenced under the reign of Alexander. The Holy Alliance, which he instituted, became an alliance of sovereigns against liberty.

The revolt which took place when Nicholas mounted the throne, planned as it was by a revolutionary society which aimed at the destruction of the ruling house, strengthened him in his autocratic and conservative tendencies. It is characteristic of Russian ignorance of all notions of freedom, that when the cry of " Long live the Constitution!" was raised, the soldiers believed that the word "Constitution" referred to the wife of the Grand Duke, Constantine, whom they thought lawfully entitled to the throne. Pastel, the leading spirit of this unripe movement for liberty, said: "I tried to gather the harvest without sowing the seed." Nicholas was the incarnation of despotism. His tyranny cut Russia off from communication with Western Europe. The severity of the censorship under his reign, the restrictions upon travel and education, and the inquisitorial methods of his police can hardly be believed by those accustomed to liberty. The most stringent regulations were made concerning tutors and governesses; their morality, including their political opinions, must be certified to by one of the universities. It was forbidden to send young men to study in Western colleges, and every obstacle was thrown in the way of foreign travel and residence. Philosophy could not be taught in the universities. This branch of knowledge was put under the control of ignorant ecclesiastics. It is easy to imagine how it flourished under such care. The press became the instrument of reaction. A newspaper which advocated the ideas of Adam Smith was regarded as dangerous, and suppressed. The daily journals themselves began to wage war against liberty of thought and all foreign innovations. It is melancholy to contemplate the misfortunes which Russia suffered under the stern rule of Nicholas. Listen to the description of Turgeneff:

Looking about, you saw venality in full feather; serfdom crushing the people down like a rock, barracks in every direction; there was no justice; threats were made of closing the universities; foreign travel was out of the question; it was impossible to procure a serious book; a gloomy cloud hung heavily over what was called the administration of literature and the sciences; informers were lurking everywhere; among the young there was no common bond, no general interest; fear and flattery were universal.

Lermontoff, the ablest Russian writer of the period, was banished three times to the Caucasus. The French Revolution of 1850 excited the indignation of Nicholas. The Hungarian uprising against Austria was sternly suppressed by his armies. He was everywhere the champion of "the existing order."

In 1815, under Alexander I., a liberal constitution had been granted to Poland, but in the latter years of that monarch, a reactionary current set in. He forbade the public sittings of the Diet, the press was gagged, and the police vexed and annoyed the people. During the reign of Nicholas an insurrection breaks out among the Poles, to regain the liberties granted to them by the constitution of Alexander. But this constitution is incompatible with autocracy. Polish patriotism is no match for Russian bayonets. Warsaw is captured, " order reigns," the old constitution is obliterated, there is no Diet, no Polish army, every thing is administered by Russian authority. The Polish language is prohibited in the schools, the universities are suppressed, five thousand Polish families are transported to the Caucasus, property worth over three hundred million francs is confiscated. In Lithuania the Roman Church is crushed and the bishops disciplined into such servility that they ask to be admitted to the Russian Church. The nuns who reject this union are banished to the forests of Siberia and subjected to unheard-of tortures.

Then comes the Crimean War, brought about by the intrigues of Nicholas. Its issue was unsuccessful, and the people, who had submitted to tyranny without a murmur while the prestige of Russia was unimpaired, now began to complain. The most frightful corruption prevailed everywhere. Anonymous pamphlets came out, denouncing the tyranny which had brought on these disasters. Listen to the following :

We have been kept long enough in serfage by the successors of the Tartar Khans. Arise and stand erect and calm before the throne of the despot ; demand of him a reckoning for the national misfortunes. Tell him boldly that his throne is not the altar of God, and that God has not condemned us forever to be his slaves.

Russia, O Czar! confided to thee the supreme power, and thou wert to her as a God upon earth. And what hast thou done? Blinded by passion and ignorance, thou hast sought nothing but power ; thou hast forgotten Russia. Thou hast consumed thy life in reviewing troops, in altering uniforms, in signing the legislative projects of ignorant charlatans. Thou hast created a despicable race of censors of the press, that thou mightest sleep in peace and never know the wants, never hear the murmurs of thy people, never listen to the voice of truth. Truth! Thou hast buried her ; thou hast rolled a great stone before the door of her sepulchre, thou hast placed a strong guard around her tomb, and in the exultation of thine heart thou hast said, "For her there is no resurrection!" Now, on the third day, Truth has arisen ; she has come forth from among the dead. Advance, O Czar! Appear at the bar of God and of history. Thou hast mercilessly trodden Truth under thy feet ; thou hast refused liberty ; at the same time thou wast enslaved by thine own passions. By thy pride and obstinacy thou hast exhausted Russia, thou hast armed the world against her. Humiliate thyself before thy brothers. Bow thy haughty forehead in the dust, implore pardon, ask counsel. Throw thyself into the arms of thy people ; there is no other way of salvation for thee.

The melancholy which overspread the entire life of Nicholas deepened under discouragement, and the flame of his life flickered out in gloom.

CHAPTER VIII.

THE REFORMS OF ALEXANDER II.

ALEXANDER II., on his accession to power, entertained the liberal ideas of Alexander I., and he was able to accomplish much more than his predecessor. Nicholas had limited the students in each university to three hundred. Alexander repealed the limitation. He reduced the excessive fees for passports, and allowed new journals to be established; the duties of individuals to the State were made less burdensome; the condition of the Jews was bettered; the children of soldiers and of sailors were *restored* to their parents. (What volumes of suggestion lie in this sentence!) The corruption during the Crimean War was such that Russian officials, who had been created into an order of nobility by Peter the Great, now fell into universal contempt. Alexander II. did something to lessen this corruption by the creation of local assemblies, called *zemstvos*.

These bodies have played quite an important part in Russian economy. Many sanguine friends of Russian institutions saw in them the true ideal of government,—local self-rule by assemblies selected by the people, with the consolidating power of autocracy binding the whole together and dealing with all national and foreign affairs. The most sanguine hopes were entertained that these bodies would regenerate the entire Russian State, restore liberty, abolish corruption, educate the people, and make of Russia an earthly paradise. It has been the tendency of the Russians to expect great things from each new reform introduced by government, and the disappointment is always keen and bitter when the performance does not come up to the prophecy. This was true of the *zemstvos*, of the Act of Emancipation, of the new tribunals and law reforms, and all the other liberal measures introduced at the beginning of the reign of Alexander. These local assemblies contain representatives from the two great classes of Russia, from the nobility (which, before emancipation, was the only land-owning class), and from the communes of the Russian peasantry, a class which constitutes three fourths of the entire population of Russia. The law provides that the preponderance in nearly all these assemblies shall remain with the nobles, but class spirit is not strong in Russia, and nobles and peasants sit side by side around the same table and conduct their business concerning education, sanitary measures, highways, fire protection, and other local matters in great harmony. The main trouble hitherto has been the lack of sufficient public interest to induce the representatives to attend. Their powers are extremely limited, they have not even the right to send a petition to the autocrat. This privilege is reserved to the assemblies of the nobles only. All matters of national politics are strictly forbidden. In one or two instances a demand for a constitution was met with

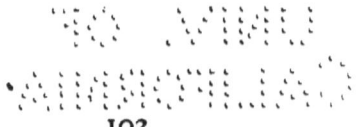
a stern reprimand, and the banishment of some of the leading spirits. A demand for the abolition of administrative exile, by which men are transported for supposed political offences without trial, was equally unsuccessful. The annual session of twenty days is insufficient to transact important business. No power is afforded to these local assemblies for enforcing their own resolutions. The governor of the province may, by his veto, delay for a year the execution of any of their measures. Meanwhile such measures are sent for examination to the central government at St. Petersburg. The financial resources of the *zemstvos* are utterly inadequate, yet with all these drawbacks, they have done much. Facilities for education were greatly increased during the first years of their activity. First in rank, in this respect, was the *zemstvo* of Viatka, where a majority of the members were peasants. The Russian *moujik* had shown an earnest desire for learning, and did all he could for the establishment of village schools, until the government interfered and took the matter out of his hands. Second among his cares was a desire for better sanitary measures in a country where medical science had been hitherto unknown. Female physicians were employed for the village communities. These were the only ones accessible within the narrow means of the *zemstvos*. But here, too, the government crippled their efforts. Women doctors were considered dangerous instruments of revolutionary propaganda, and the government limited the number that might be employed. Savings banks, drainage, and a system of mutual fire-insurance also occupied their attention. In a small way the *zemstvos* have done

much good, so much, indeed, that the government has been continually withdrawing the narrow powers which it formerly conceded to them.

Another reform which marked the first years of the reign of Alexander, was the abolition of many of the restrictions of the censorship. " Speech, that was long restrained by police and censorial regulations, now flows smoothly, harmoniously, and majestically, like a mighty river that has just been freed from ice." Periodicals soon appeared with articles on trade and political economy. Even official corruption was discussed.

But these new concessions granted to liberty were soon withdrawn. Alexander II. followed in the footsteps of Alexander I.; he was liberal in the beginning, but reactionary and tyrannical in his later years.

Another important reform, introduced at the beginning of his reign, was the establishment of the new tribunals. The procedure of the Russian courts had been secret, written, venal, and inquisitorial. The police had entire control of criminal matters. The fate of suitors commonly depended upon the length of their purses. The judges, without exception, supplemented their meagre salaries with bribes. The most honest judge was he who took from both sides and decided as he thought right. A great change was made by Alexander. The proceedings became public, higher salaries were given, the profession of the bar came into life, and criminal causes were tried by jury. Still the right to banish for suspected crimes against the State was not affected, and later, Alexander recalled much that he had given. Politi-

cal trials are secret ; they are confided to military tribunals ; none but an officer of the army may represent the
accused. Even the ordinary criminal judges receive, for
the most part, provisional and probationary appointments.
The condition of the courts and the perversions of justice
in recent years will be described hereafter.

But the great reform of Alexander was the abolition of
serfdom. It is interesting to trace the history of this remarkable institution, and to consider its character as well
as the character of the people upon whom it was imposed.
The *moujik*, or peasant, is par excellence the typical
Russian. At the time of the Tartar invasion, the
peasants were the Krestianin, or Christians, who remained
uncorrupted, free from the infusion of Tartar blood and
Tartar infidelity. In the opinion of the Slavophils, the
peasantry of Russia contains the great undeveloped
potentiality of Russian growth. It is the "unhatched
egg"; the "unawakened Sphynx," which hides within
its breast the undivulged secret of the future. Endowed
with considerable natural intelligence, but wholly lacking
even the most rudimentary instruction, the peasant
is like the giant of the Russian legend " Ilya of Mur-
oum," who has never been able to show his power and
talent. Reduced to servitude, he has been bound to
the soil and loaded with chains, and even when freed
at last, he has no longer the use of his limbs nor the
knowledge of his power. The causes of serfdom are not
hard to find. It was not an Asiatic importation. It was
an institution which grew up with the Grand Principality
of Moscow. In the very early history of the Russians, as

early as the time of Iaroslaf, or even before that, slaves were taken in battle and became the absolute property of their captors, but the origin of serfdom is not to be traced to this source. The serfs were originally the free cultivators of the soil. With the growth of military power the peasant naturally sank in the social scale. The history of serfdom in Russia is the same as that of similar institutions in countries which are at the same time agricultural and military. While Russian unity was being cemented under the Princes of Moscow, the followers of the Prince, the nobles and the small landholders had to be equipped and properly supplied for war. The labor of the cultivators of the soil was brought into use for this purpose, but there was no limitation confining the peasant to any particular tract or any particular master; he might change masters every year upon St. George's Day; land had little value except that given it by the peasants who dwelt upon it. The larger the estate the more productive was cultivation, and the less severe were the exactions of the master. The result was that the peasants abandoned the lesser proprietors and entered the service of the wealthier nobles, and thus a large portion of the smaller land owners, who followed the Prince in his wars, were unable to equip and support themselves properly, and the military service suffered. To remedy this, Boris Godunof prohibited the peasants from changing their masters, and fixed them to the glebe; he afterward modified this decree and permitted changes from one small land owner to another, but this liberty was again revoked at a later period.

Once fixed to the soil, the peasant soon lost all civil rights.

When Peter the Great provided that every noble should remain in the service of the State during his entire life, a natural corollary of this arrangement was that he should be supported by the labor of his serfs, and we find that the power of the master, during Peter's reign, was confirmed and strengthened. The State abandoned to the landed proprietor the civil administration and police power in his domains. The noble became the agent of the State for the government of his serfs.

Peter III. freed the nobility from the obligation of life-long service to the State; the logical sequence of this would have been to free the serfs from their corresponding obligations, but no such step was taken. In the reign of Catharine II., the power of the master was still further strengthened; he could send his serfs to Siberia at will. From the reforms of subsequent reigns the serfs received no benefit.

Serfdom was almost entirely confined to the dominions of the ancient Principality of Moscow. It prevailed to the greatest extent in the neighborhood of the ancient Russian capital. It did not exist in the extreme North, nor was it found among the Tartars, nor did it ever gain a firm foothold in Siberia. The peasantry were about equally divided into two great classes—crown peasants or serfs belonging to the State, and serfs belonging to individual proprietors. At the time of the emancipation there were about twenty-two millions of each class; there was also a much smaller number of household servants and serfs belonging to the appanages. The serfs belonging to the crown enjoyed greater liberty than the other classes. During the entire continuance of this remarkable system, the little agricultural villages, composed of these serfs, retained their original Slavonic form of communal government ; they had their *mir* to settle their internal disputes, and they tilled in common the land which they held.

This was also true with many of the serfs belonging to the nobles, but there was no general rule upon the subject. Their condition depended largely upon the caprice of the masters. The peasants belonging to the large proprietors were generally the most fortunate. The great noble, Cheremetief, had among his serfs men who became millionnaires. There were two systems greatly in vogue for securing the labor of serfs. First, the Corvée, under which the master was entitled to the labor of the serfs three days in each week, the remainder of the time being given to the peasant to cultivate his own land for his own support. Second, the Obrok system, which was more favorable to the peasant. Under this he was permitted to enjoy his liberty and to follow whatever trade or occupation he desired, upon condition of paying a certain annual sum to his proprietor. The household servants bore a much closer resemblance to our own slaves; these were not attached to the soil, and were sold and treated in much the same manner as the negroes in the South. Up to the beginning of the present century there was a regular class of slave-dealers, and advertisements of sales appeared in the public press and in handbills in the streets.

Wallace gives many instances: "In this house one can buy a coachman and a Dutch cow about to calve"; "To be sold—three coachmen, well trained and handsome, and three girls," etc. Alexander I. prohibited these advertisements, but the traffic continued. Even in the case of peasants bound to the glebe, their condition depended more upon the character of their masters than upon any protection afforded to them by the law. Serfdom bore with crushing weight upon all the institutions of Russia. The wasteful system of agriculture which it encouraged, the violation of human rights which it sanctioned, and the moral degradation which it imposed upon the community, find their best parallel in our own Southern States before the war. The nobles themselves, however, were more keenly alive to these disadvantages than the slave-owners of the South. Public opinion was gradually ripening for a change in the system. Russia had its " Uncle Tom's Cabin " in the " Recollections of a Sportsman," by Turgeneff, and in " Anton the Unfortunate " of Irigorovitch. The disasters of the Crimean War were generally laid to the charge of the corrupt social organization fostered by this baleful institution, and a large part of the proprietors co-operated heartily with the Czar in his projects of reform.

While something may be attributed to the liberal and humanitarian views of Alexander, the main cause of his great scheme of emancipation was the financial disadvantage of serf labor. The experience of the world everywhere is that no such system can be made highly productive, that the proper incentives to industry are wanting, and that there is always more or less danger of a social catastrophe in the shape of a servile war. Alexander repeatedly said that it was better to reform from above than from below, and he appeared to regard the danger of insurrection as formidable. He proceeded by gradual steps, and the emancipation was accomplished in a masterly manner. So far as crown peasants were concerned, there was little difficulty; there was little to do but declare them free, to remove the restrictions on their right to come and go, to acquire land, and dispose of their goods. The Lithuanians, who had shown a disposition to aid Alexander in his project, were also authorized to free their serfs.

The great difficulty with proprietary serfage was that granting liberty alone was not enough, for the serf, although subject to his master, had rights in the land. The peasant's maxim was: "We are yours, but the land is ours." To grant mere liberty to the peasant and to leave the land to his master would be to form an immense proletariat. All obligations upon the part of the master would be removed and the peasant would still be completely at his mercy. A system of peonage would be established worse than serfdom. It was necessary to secure to the peasants at least part of the property they had cultivated, and to strengthen the village communities as a bulwark against pauperism.

By the edict of 1861 the peasants were made free, and the lands actually occupied by them were granted to them. These varied in quantity generally in inverse ratio to their fertility; the average was about nine acres

to each male head of a family. The serfs were to pay
a perpetual rent for the lands granted to them, but they
were authorized, in their discretion, to purchase these
lands in fee. Four fifths of the purchase-money was
loaned to them by the government, and they were to re-
pay the amount loaned by a series of annual payments,
extending over fifty years. Most of the peasants availed
themselves of this right of purchase, and they are still en-
gaged in the task of paying for the lands conceded to
them by the Act of Emancipation. The village government of the *mir*, with the *starosta* at its head, was confirmed. These villages were combined in the *volost* or
Canton under the *starschina.*

During the emancipation many disputes occurred between the peasants and their former masters in regard to
the amount and value of the land which they were to
receive. Reports had been circulated among them that
the Czar had made them a free gift of the soil which they
cultivated, and there was great dissatisfaction when they
found that they were compelled to pay for land which
they had always considered their own ; but the tribunals
to which the government had entrusted the delicate question of appraisement performed their office with great
skill, and the discontent was finally allayed.

Much credit is due to the old masters for the disinterested manner in which these "Arbitrators of the Peace,"
selected from the ranks of the nobility, performed their
functions. Enfranchisement was effected in Russia in a
manner far more skilful than in our own country, where it
was accomplished through the terrible agency of civil war.

Yet the Russian people have been perhaps less satisfied with its results.

Subsequent investigation has been made by the government as to the effects of emancipation upon the peasants. While the ultimate results can scarcely be otherwise than good, the temporary inconveniences were very great. The serfs have been compelled to work harder than ever to pay for the land which they had always cultivated and regarded as their own. The complete ignorance of the Russian *moujik* has laid him open to vices which serfdom did much to suppress. Drunkenness has probably increased since emancipation. The peasants are now free, of course, from the former claims of their masters; they used to be obliged to work for him three days each week; they could not change their residence without his permission; the master could sell or mortgage the land to which they were attached, permit or forbid them to marry, and inflict upon them corporal punishment. All these things are past.

Under the new system the land is not granted to the peasant personally, but to the village community, by which it is held in common.

This communal system has its advantages and its drawbacks. The government collects the taxes, not from individuals, but from the *mir*. In many communities the taxes are greater than the rental value of the land. In these places the peasants eke out the deficiency by industrial pursuits, by the manufacture of articles which are sold in the cities and in other parts of the empire. Many leave their villages and ply their trades elsewhere, paying to the commune for this privilege their ratable proportion of the tax. The rigorous passport system, which prevails in Russia, enables the *mir* to keep them in its power, even though they may travel great distances in search of work. But in the most fertile parts of Russia, including the great zone of the Black Land, the produce of the soil is more than sufficient to pay the tax and to afford the means of subsistence to the peasants who cultivate it. The land is not farmed in common, but is divided among the villagers, at periods varying, in different communities, from one to fifteen years. This distribution is made by the village assembly, which meets in council in the open air, generally upon Sunday, in front of the church.

By this system, the peasants are protected from pauperism. Each peasant has his own plot of land, and the means of gaining a livelihood. Of this he cannot be permanently deprived, even by his own improvidence. But the system has its disadvantage in discouraging individual enterprise. There is no motive for permanent improvement of the land, when the man who makes it cannot avail himself of the benefit of such improvements. It is a system which encourages mediocrity, and constitutes a bar to any great economical progress. These communes are often extremely tyrannical. If one of their members is more prudent and successful than the rest and saves something, his fellow villagers often compel him to disgorge, by fines, capriciously imposed, or by other vexatious restraints upon his liberty. It is common for the more prosperous peasants to feign poverty. Sometimes a *moujik* will buy the right to leave his commune. The fact that the *mir*, as a whole, is responsible to the government for all taxes, as well as for the purchase-money of the land (which has been loaned by the State), gives it great power in controlling the actions of its members. A peasant may be publicly whipped or banished to Siberia by his fellow villagers assembled in council.

A commission of inquiry, instituted by the government attributes the slow growth of agriculture to the communal system, and yet if these communities were more intelligent, and farmed the land together instead of dividing it for short periods of time, it might be found that ownership and cultivation in common were well adapted to these vast plains, where farming ought to be carried on upon a large scale to be most productive, and where the use of improved agricultural machinery could be undertaken more effectively by the commune than by a single individual. Conducted by intelligence, coöperation is no more impossible in agricultural enterprises than in manufactures, where it has been conducted with such success through the agency of corporations. It is the union of this joint ownership with dense ignorance, which, in Russia, retards the advancement of industry.

Politically, the consequences of emancipation have been very slight. It has not affected, thus far, the power of the despotism. Economically, it has added something to the stimulus to production, but this is still greatly restrained. Its moral effects have been most important. They can be seen in greater freedom of conscience and individual responsibility, in the improvement in the condition of the women, in the weakening of patriarchal institutions, and in the growth of greater individualism. Many of the peasants have been able, from their savings, to purchase small tracts from their former masters, which they cultivate upon their individual account. In the more fertile districts land has increased in value. The nobles have been the greatest losers by the change. They had an easier life of it while serfdom existed. Since its abolition they have had to give up their traditional indolence and dependence upon the labor of others. They have been compelled to shift for themselves. The skilful and provident have held their own, while the shiftless and careless have lost their all. The land of Russia is gradually passing from the hands of the nobles who used to own it all, into the hands of the merchants, and the *moujiks.*

Individual ownership and joint ownership being found side by side in Russia, if the government will withhold its hand, the type which is found best adapted to surrounding conditions will undoubtedly prevail. This non-interference, however, is a thing which can never be predicated of the Russian administration. Its tendency is to direct the most minute affairs of life.

After emancipation was accomplished, the nobles, in consideration of the sacrifices which they had undergone in being deprived of their serfs, demanded reforms in their own favor. They claimed for themselves a larger degree of liberty. Quite radical measures were considered, but the discussions were soon met with police interference, and a stern reprimand from the Czar. The Poles asked for a constitution; there were great public demonstrations of unarmed men which could only be dispersed by the muskets of the soldiery. All Poles compromised in the demonstrations were commanded to sell their estates; the use of the Polish language and even the Polish alphabet was forbidden. Catholic churches were closed; whole villages were destroyed. Poland did not share in the new institutions which Alexander granted elsewhere.

Yet it was undoubtedly the intention of the Czar to continue still further, along the lines laid out by himself, the reforms which he had begun; and it is now well known that his assassination took place on the very day when he had resolved to convoke a national assembly composed of representatives from the provincial *zemstvos*.

It is not strange, therefore, that when Alexander III., his son and successor, stood before the mutilated corpse of his father, and learned for the first time the particulars of the liberal measures which that father had projected, he should have adopted the stern reactionary policy which has continued with little change down to the present day.

CHAPTER IX.

THE DESPOTISM OF ALEXANDER III.

To the eyes of Alexander III. modern ideas were responsible for the nihilism and corruption of the rising generation. The conclusion was plain that the patriarchal Byzantine orthodox Church and the patriarchal paternal autocracy were the only salvation for Russia, and, through Russia, for the future of the world. Nationalism—the exclusion of every Western element and influence—was to be the talisman of this regeneration. The political and religious instruction of Alexander's early manhood had been confided to Pobedonostseff, who in 1880 became the Procurator of the Holy Synod, —the political head of the State Church,—a man distinguished alike for cool, calculating policy and unbending fanaticism. Under his guidance Alexander, a man of personal honesty, conscientiousness, and purity of life, became convinced of the providential destiny of the Eastern Church to regenerate the West, and entered upon the gloomy career of bigotry and despotism which still remain the dominating characteristics of the autocracy.

Nowhere else in the world is there the same control by the central government, not only of local affairs, but of the most minute particulars of individual life. The people are treated as if they were minors, incapable of doing anything for themselves. " Neither a chair in a college nor a bed in a hospital can be endowed without the intervention of the State."

The Russian remains all his life " like a soldier in his regiment, who marches, halts, advances, retreats, lifts his leg or his foot at the command of the instructing sergeant." Education, the press, and the intelligence and virtue of the people are all stifled by this blighting influence.

Thanks to the aid of the rapid auxiliaries furnished by modern science ; thanks to steam and electricity, business has been more and more concentrated in the hands of the Ministers. . . . The Russian administration has become like an endless chain, along which business has moved mechanically, slowly, going up and down, from office to office, to the great injury of the interests of the country (Leroy-Beaulieu).

First, let us consider the policy of Russia in respect to education. So completely is the spirit of Russian government opposed to liberal culture, that the universities there are not, as with us, simple institutions of learning ; they are the centres of all that there is of Russian agitation. The university students are almost the only educated persons in the empire who are not restrained by the caution of age or the selfishness of station and property. They are almost the only class who discuss, with any freedom, political affairs. Hence they are continually subject to the interference of the police ; their clubs and unions, and even their social meetings, are frequently dispersed. Inquiries are made of porters and of the lodging-house keepers, as to the habits of the students, whom they entertain, what hours they keep, and what company, and how they express themselves. An examination of their books and papers is frequently made by the police in their absence. The police inspector appointed by the government may, with the approbation of the curator, expel a student without inquiry. He can deny scholarships at will, or refuse permission to any student to give private lessons, thus taking away the student's means of livelihood. Students are often banished for mere breaches of scholastic discipline, the banishment being sometimes permanent exile. The police frequently ask for the names of all who have been brought before the university tribunals, for the purpose of adding exile or other government punishment to that of the university. The law of 1881 directs the councils of the universities to try all students who have been *tried and acquitted* by ordinary courts, or who have expiated their offences against the civil law by a term of imprisonment. If the police certify that the young man has acted out of pure thoughtlessness, the council may acquit or expel him at its discretion, but should they impute perverse intent, the council *must* expel him.

When we come to secondary instruction, we find that even the schoolboy, from ten to seventeen years of age, may be banished for holding wrong political opinions. History, Russian literature, and even geography, are discouraged by the Minister of Instruction, on account of their *dangerous* tendencies. In the seminaries the classics are almost the only things taught. Nine boys out of ten are dropped at examinations. Such a system, as Stepniak says, is not a test of proficiency, it is a "massacre of the innocents," a plan for depriving the vast majority of all chance of a useful career. The "real" or scientific schools are few in number, and the instruction afforded by them is imperfect. A more complete course is given in what is known as the supplementary section, which, however, is limited to two years. The instruction even here is quite superficial. So inadequate are these schools to meet the demand for education, that out of a thousand applicants not more than two hundred are received, but still the government forbids new colleges, lest, being recruited from the poorer classes, they should become infected with socialism.

One would think that even a despotism might encourage primary instruction; yet in Russia, elementary education is so restricted that it confers but little benefit upon its possessor. Prior to the emancipation in 1861 there was scarcely any instruction in Russia of this character. A considerable number of the schools which were supposed to exist, and which were paid for out of the exchequer, existed only "on paper"; that is to say, the officers in charge of them simply took the money and put it in their pockets. The reports furnished to the department were simply fictions. Some primary instruction, however, was given by private effort. Finally, in 1864, control of elementary instruction was given to the *zemstvos*, or local assemblies. But the revenues of these bodies, for all local purposes, industrial, sanitary, and educational, was only one twentieth of the entire revenue. They could do but little; still they started training-schools for teachers, but the Minister of Public Instruction vetoed these proposed normal colleges, deeming them a means of political contamination. After the German war he yielded this point reluctantly. Then, in 1870, he concluded that the primary schools were sources of political propaganda, and he created a sort of private police to watch the teachers. The character of the instruction and its political tendencies, with "observations and conjectures," were to be reported. The numerous interferences, encouraged by the government, render the position of a teacher unbearable. The regulation of 1874 limits instruction in the primary schools to sacred history, reading, writing, and the first four rules of arithmetic. The minister refused the petition of the *zemstvos* to permit the teaching of geography and Russian grammar. In the schools of Finland and Poland the Russian language only is taught; the natives cannot learn to read and write their own tongue. The interference of government inspectors is always for the purpose of *suppressing* instruction. In 1879 the *zemstvo* of Riazan thanked the inspectors for having "abstained from using the means at their disposal to thwart the *zemstvo* in their efforts to promote primary instruction and increase the usefulness of the village schools."

The little prosperity that attended primary education was derived from the care of these local assemblies, but in 1884 the schools were taken from the *zemstvos* altogether, and placed in the hands of the ignorant Russian clergy, and Pobedonostseff undertook the extraordinary job of dismissing some scores of thousands of village school teachers and appointing priests in their stead. The priests of Russia are notoriously a worthless class. Such is the influence of Russian government on popular instruction.

The despotism is as relentless with the press as with education. Since all knowledge is a threat to tyranny, the only safe course is to gag the instruments by which it can be spread. The censorship is more stringent now than it was in the time of Peter the Great. Peter tortured and put to death the opponents of his reforms, but he encouraged general literature. So did Catharine the Second at the beginning of her reign, but when the French Revolution laid the foundations of popular government in Europe, this liberality disappeared; editors were imprisoned and exiled for advocating ideas which Catharine herself had formerly professed. During the stern reign of Nicholas, the iron hand of autocracy crushed out all the elements of growth. Every manuscript, every newspaper article had to be submitted to the censors before publication. This censorship still prevails in every part of Russia except Moscow and St. Petersburg, and under its withering influence the press is practically dead.

In 1865, during the era of reform, the corrective censure was instituted in these two cities. Papers may be printed without first submitting them to the censors, but if any thing offensive is published, the journal is warned, and after three warnings it is suppressed, or the minister may suspend publication for three months, without warning, or stop sales in the streets, or forbid advertisements.

No judicial inquiry is necessary; he simply does this at his own pleasure. Absolute suppression at first required a judicial inquiry, but this was too inconvenient. The emperor on one occasion, at a ball, ordered two newspapers suppressed. The minister usually sends a note to the different editors against the publication of various matters which he considers it undesirable for the public to know, such as "the disturbances among the university students," accounts of "political trials," etc. Journals may *praise*, but must not *criticise*, the acts of the government in Bulgaria; they must not publish comments on the decisions of the *zemstvos* (their own local representative bodies); they are forbidden to publish "the report of the special commission of the Jews," articles on "peasant emigration," articles on "the relation of peasants to other landowners," etc., etc., etc. Sometimes newspapers seem to be suppressed from mere caprice. In some parts of Russia, where the preventive censure exists, the government requires the submission of all articles to a censor living in a remote district, involving sometimes fifteen days' delay. Daily papers cannot well appear under such conditions. The Tiflis *Phalanga* was suppressed for merely *presenting to the censor* a drawing considered unsuitable. In 1884 the editor of the *Dielo* was ordered to sell his journal to a Mr. Wolfman, a reactionist, with the statement that if he did not, the censors would refuse every article presented. Among the works suppressed by Russian censorship are Lecky's " History of European Morals,"Hobbe's "Leviathan," and Haeckel's "History of Creation."

By a refinement of tyranny, only possible in Russia, a decree of the censure, passed in 1876, forbade the millions of inhabitants of Little Russia to print, sell, or circulate any works in their own tongue, either original or translated. Even the circulation of foreign books in the same language is forbidden. The · purpose of this decree was to compel the people of Little Russia to adopt the language of Moscow and St. Petersburg. A whole literature has thus been annihilated, and the dialects of the Ukraine, in which the lightest and most graceful part of Russian genius has expressed itself, have thus been condemned to eternal silence, and the people kept in enforced ignorance of all written speech, unless they would consent to learn a language other than their own.

But it is in its judicial system that the Russian government tramples most ruthlessly upon individual rights. Whenever the police deem it best, they steal noiselessly through the streets and alleys surrounding a private dwelling in the dead of night, creep in silence up the stairway, gain admittance under some false pretence, and invade every room in the house, waking the sleeping occupants. Each member of the household is given in charge of a policeman, every thing in the house is then turned topsy-turvy, books, papers, private letters are carefully inspected—nothing is secret. It is not necessary that the police should have any evidence for these searches; an anonymous charge or a mere suspicion is enough. Houses have been inspected *seven times in a single day*, sometimes *every house in a street* is overhauled. If any thing is discovered to excite the suspicion of the police, an arrest follows, and the supposed culprit is sent to the House of Preventive Detention.   There he awaits his trial for weeks and months, and sometimes for years. He is brought out occasionally for examination. If he confesses nothing, he is sent back "to reflect." Sometimes the wrong man is arrested and confined a year or two before the mistake is discovered. Ponomareff was imprisoned thus for three years.

The solitary confinement to which prisoners are subjected in this House of Detention is often fatal. Consumption, insanity, and suicide frequently occur. The examination of the prisoners and witnesses is dragged to an interminable length ; in the trial of the one hundred and ninety-three (one of the celebrated cases), the examination lasted *four years*. Over seven hundred persons, mostly witnesses, were kept in the jail during this time. The prosecutor said that only twenty persons deserved punishment, yet there were seventy-three who died from suicide or from the effects of confinement. Confessions are frequently extorted by threats of death or of incarceration in one of the terrible fortresses of Russia. Prisoners are deprived of the means of reading and writing, to extort evidence from them. The trials are like the preliminary proceedings. In 1872 all political cases were withdrawn from the ordinary tribunals and "assigned to particular Senatorial chambers," appointed by the Emperor. This court could be relied upon to decide in compliance with his will. The offence of propagating revolutionary doctrines is punished by penal servitude for from five to nine years ; the punishment is the same as that for robbery or unaggravated murder. A number of young girls who had been studying at Zurich became impressed with the necessity of a larger liberty and greater equality for the oppressed lower classes of Russia ; and knowing that they could reach the class whom they aimed to instruct in no other way, they took places in the cotton factories of Moscow, and taught their fellow-operators fraternity and socialism. This was unaccompanied by violence or any threat of violence, yet they received the terrible sentence of penal servitude, which was afterwards commuted to perpetual exile in Siberia. When the so-called Terrorist period was inaugurated by the use of dynamite, and an attack was made upon the life of the Emperor, the trial of political offenders was taken away from the civil tribunals and committed to officers of the army. Even the counsel for the prisoner must be a military officer, whose rank and fortune were wholly at the mercy of the government. He was not allowed access to the depositions until a few hours before the trial. Men have been judged, condemned, and executed in a single day. Others have suffered death before their identity could be proved. Men have been arrested at night, taken to a private house, tried there by officers, and hanged the next day. Mlodetski was sentenced and executed without any judicial inquiry. It appears from the strongest evidence that these military judges have strictly obeyed their masters, and have simply executed sentences prescribed beforehand. In one case the death penalty was imposed as a *cumulative* sentence for a number of crimes, *each punishable by a few years' penal servi-*

tude. General Mrovinsky and others were sentenced to banishment because *they failed to discover* the Petersburg mine. Sometimes the secret informant is rewarded by the confiscated property of the condemned. Sometimes the judges demand instructions from St. Petersburg before rendering judgment. Government officials publicly boast that the tribunals will do whatever they desire. Even the so-called public trials could not be attended without a permit from the presiding judge. They were held in small apartments, which were so filled with witnesses and officers of court that the public could not enter. Then the right of the accused to a public trial was limited to the presence of three witnesses, and later, this was restricted to one person, who must be either his wife, his parent, or his child. Newspapers cannot publish their own accounts of trials, but must copy the official reports. After the murder of the Czar, all trials were heard with closed doors, the nearest of kin to the accused were excluded, and even the inhabitants of the next dwelling had often no suspicion that a political trial was going on.

But a trial is little more than a formality ; if the accused is acquitted, the police may arrest him at once and doom him to exile, without hearing, upon mere " administrative order."

The secret council of ten in the republic of Venice has long been set before the imagination of men as perhaps the blackest type in history of that irresponsible and arbitrary tyranny which condemns men to punishment upon secret charges preferred by unknown accusers without process of law, and often for no crime, but upon reasons of supposed state policy alone; yet there is in Russia to-day a system founded upon the same principles, and quite as repugnant to all ideas of justice. Men who have never been tried, nor perhaps even accused, but who are simply *suspected* by the police, are often, without any inquiry whatever, simply as a matter of arbitrary will, placed under so-called " police supervision." This, to be effective, must be at some point distant from the residence of the man suspected, so that his friends and his supposed fellow-conspirators can have no access to him ; hence we have a system of so-called administrative exile, by which any person, innocent or guilty, may be sent at the pleasure of the police to any part of the great Russian Empire. Until recently the term of exile might be prolonged indefinitely. Indeed, the secret police considered that men who suffered from this kind of tyranny were not apt to become reconciled, and they were not often permitted to return. This exile frequently follows an acquittal in court, in cases where no proof of guilt can be procured. This system was not formally recognized by the code until 1879, after an attempt was made upon the Czar's life. At that time, six generals were appointed over six districts of the empire, with the right to exile by administrative order " all persons whose stay might be considered prejudicial to the public welfare, to imprison at discretion, to suppress or suspend any journal, to take such measures as might be necessary for the public safety." The general terms of their authority were in language almost identical with the power given to the Roman dictators, to see to it " that the common-

wealth should suffer no harm." There are instances of
exile without proof or trial to the desert wastes of Eastern Siberia. Men have been banished simply because
they belonged to "a dangerous family." Men have been
sent to the frozen North because the police have confused
their names with those of others whom they have suspected. Often the discovery of the mistake did not lead to a
revocation. We have instances of exile where the order
itself declares that they have been found innocent of any
crime.

Witness the following :

The gendarmerie department of Moscow accused Mr. Isidor
Goldsmith and his wife Sophia of having come to Moscow intent
on founding a central revolutionary committee. After a minute domiciliary search and an examination for the discovery
of proofs, the charges brought against the before-mentioned
persons were found to be quite without justification. *Conse-
quently* the Minister of the Interior and the Chief of the Gendarmerie decree that Isidor Goldsmith and Sophia his wife be
transported to Archangelsk, and there placed under the supervision of the local police.

The exile never knows his accusers, and is often wholly
ignorant of the reason for which he is transported. These
exiles are forbidden to teach, lecture, print, photograph,
practise medicine, sell books or papers, act as librarian, or
serve in the government employment, such occupations
being considered " dangerous to the State." The local
government may veto any other occupation which is considered undesirable. The exiles are allowed six to eight
rubles a month (about $5.00) for their support, if they

are of noble birth, otherwise only half of that amount. Many of them find it scarcely possible to support life in a strange country with these restrictions. All their letters are examined by the police. Even their literary societies are broken up. It is dangerous for others to become intimate with them. The report of an able Russian officer to the government contains the following remarkable words :

From the experience of past years, and my own personal observation, I have arrived at the conclusion that administrative exile for political causes tends rather to exasperate a man and infect him with perverse ideas, than to correct him (correction being the officially declared object of exile). The change from a life of ease to a life of privation, from life in the bosom of society to separation from all society, from an activity more or less active to an enforced inaction,—all this produces an effect so disastrous that often, especially of late, there have occurred among the exiles cases of madness, of suicide, and attempted suicide.

Men have been exiled in this manner and sent on foot with gangs of malefactors to the country of the Yakoutes, savages of Eastern Siberia, where they must live in the filthy and wretched huts of these half-naked barbarians, whose language they cannot speak, whose food they cannot eat. Few men survive this transportation more than a few years.

Leroy-Beaulieu thus speaks of this system of exile by order of the Police of State :

No engine of despotism, not even, perhaps, the Spanish

Inquisition, has cut down so many human beings and crushed so many lives, since none has ever acted more discreetly and with less noise. There is no list of martyrs so long as that of this State Chancellery. The number of its victims, of every rank, of every age, of both sexes, is the harder to estimate, since, in place of public *autos-da-fé*, it surrounded them almost always with mystery, and hid them in the silent snows of Siberia, and being able to get rid of them without having blood upon its hands, and without hearing their cries, it was itself so much the less scrupulous and compassionate.

The State Police has remained mistress of the right to imprison, to bury, to banish whomsoever it desires. Under Alexander III., as under Alexander II., the High Police remains sovereign, independent of justice and the courts, and has no account to render, except to its chief or to the Emperor.

Another law provides that administrative exile shall not exceed five years, and that it must be approved by a commission composed of two delegates from the Ministry of the Interior and two from the Ministry of Justice. This commission *may, if they choose,* ask the accused to appear and defend himself. As a guaranty for liberty this discretionary formality is absolutely illusory. The sum total of injustice and misery will not be materially lessened in any such way.

But even where there has been a trial by the courts, very little is settled by the judgment. The fatal point is, after conviction, to know where the condemned shall go, for there is all the difference in the world between being sent to the mines of Siberia and to the fortresses of Russia. The friends of the condemned importune the government to send him to Siberia. His wife, his mother, or his betrothed make long journeys to St. Petersburg and clamor everywhere for this mitigation of sentence, and the condemned is happy indeed if he is sent to that terrible land of chains and ice. One would think it was hard enough to be condemned to labor in the mines, yet the Siberian prisoner thinks it a privilege, for the hardest toil is a lighter punishment than solitary confinement within the walls of a prison. The terms of imprisonment vary from twenty to thirty-five years. Political prisoners are treated with greater severity than other convicts. Other prisons have outer walls upon three sides only, and front upon the street ; political prisons are built in the middle of a court, surrounded on every side by walls. Vivid accounts are given of the outrages to which the prisoners are subjected. As one of them expressed it : " We are beaten twice a day and fed once."

But these prisons, in a land where the cold is sixty degrees below zero, are deemed a paradise to the great prisons of Russia, in which political offenders are confined as in a living tomb. The best among the latter is the central prison, at Novo Belgorod. This is a great penitentiary for the worst grade of malefactors as well as political convicts. The common criminals live and work together, but the political offenders are doomed to solitary confinement. Each lives alone in silence in his little cell. Even their exercise is taken separately, so that they cannot meet. The brigands and murderers confined with them are treated with greater consideration. In July, 1878, the political prisoners refused to eat, because they

were denied the right to work in the prison and in the
workshops with the rest.   For eight days they tasted
nothing, and became so weak that they could not rise
from their beds, until the governor-general promised compliance with their request, which promise he afterwards
violated.   Yet these men had been guilty of nothing but
the simple propagation of the doctrines of socialism.
There had been no violence nor breach of law other than
teaching this heresy.   These prisoners, contrary to the
laws of the prison, were put in irons on the slightest pretence, or thrown into the punishment cells, cages so small
that men cannot stand in them, or deprived of books at
the caprice of their brutal jailors, and beds taken away
even from the sick.   Once, when a prisoner who had
served his probation term was put in irons against the
rules of the prison, a petition was sent to the governor-
general, who, in his decision, admitted that the director
had no right to put the prisoner in irons, but, neverthe-
less, ordered all the prisoners who had signed the petition
to be manacled, on the ground that they had insulted the
director by their complaint, and he gave to each of them
from one to three days in the black hole.   The men imprisoned at Novo Belgorod had done nothing but distribute
socialistic pamphlets.   When the work of nihilism went
to greater lengths, and violence was resorted to, these
prisoners, who were wholly innocent, were made to feel
the consequences.   Their books were taken away from
them, they were put in irons, their relatives were exiled
to distant provinces and sent to Siberia; even the ven-
tilating orifices of their cells were closed, so that they

could scarcely breathe. Of young men in the prime of life, many died. Within four years, out of fourteen prisoners confined in the rear cells to the right, five went mad, and filled the prison with their howlings. Some died insane in their cells.

But this prison is used only for lighter punishment, for those who have not been guilty of crimes of violence. Those charged with heavier offences are immured within the walls of Schlüsselberg, or in the fortress of Peter and Paul. To what doom they are condemned in the first of these great silent tombs, no one knows, for the voice of those who are buried there has never reached the outside world. For those who pass within its accursed walls, the superscription of the infernal gates is written thereon : " All hope abandon, ye who enter here." Their destiny is fixed forever; there is no hope, no word, no return. But the fortress of Peter and Paul, situated, as it is, in the very capital of the nation, cannot be so completely isolated. This is the great Bastile of Russia. It has its traditions like that of the Man in the Iron Mask. This fortress is under military government, every attendant is a soldier, and the prisoners are forbidden to speak, not only to each other, but to their jailers. The jailers visit their cells in pairs to prevent collusion. They are immured in alternate cells, so that they may not communicate with each other by raps or signals. Spies are placed in the intervening chambers, to extract testimony which cannot be otherwise secured. Men have been confined in this fortress many years and no one knew where they were. The identity of these prisoners is concealed by a simple numeral, and their names are often unknown to the jailers who attend them.

The effect of this crushing despotism on the natural life of Russia is thus graphically stated by Stepniak.

Despotism has stricken with sterility the high hopes to which the splendid awakening of the first half of the century gave birth. Mediocrity reigns supreme. . . . All the leaders of our zemstvos, modest as are their functions, belong to an older generation.   The living forces of later generations have been buried by the government in Siberian snows and Esquimaux villages.   It is worse than the pest.   A pest comes and goes ; but the government has oppressed the country for twenty years, and may go on oppressing it for who knows how many years longer.   The pest kills indiscriminately, but the present régime chooses its victims from the flower of the nation, taking all on whom depend its future and glory.   It is not a political party whom they crush ; it is a nation of a hundred millions whom they stifle.

This is what is done in Russia under the Czars ; this is the price at which the government buys its miserable existence.

One would think that the more intelligent people of Russia would abandon a country thus infected ; but even this poor privilege is denied them ; they cannot lawfully leave the empire, nor even their own town, without the consent of their government.

Every Russian found without a passport is an outlaw, to be hunted down by the authorities.

In 1879 the police of Tiflis, having received an order to arrest for expulsion all persons without passports living in the city, there was a general flight among workmen, small merchants, coachmen, and servants, so that from lack of hands a thrifty population suddenly found itself in the greatest difficulty. Instead of heeding the demands of the police, those interested fled by thousands, so as not to be brought back to their homes by chain-gangs, as the law prescribed. Money only could obtain relief from the hardships of the law.

Political trials have shown that many unfortunates have been cast into the party of anarchy and revolution by the lack of a passport or the loss of their papers.[1]

The government always prohibits permanent emigration. Anywhere the Russian may go he can never lose his citizenship. Russia does not admit the right of any subject to abandon his allegiance, and will not permit any naturalization elsewhere to interfere with her claims upon his obedience.

We can foretell the fate of liberal institutions if subjected to Russian domination, not only by the treatment of Poland but also by the course that has been followed in recent years in respect to Finland. This Grand Duchy passed from Sweden to Russia in the year 1800 during the wars of Napoleon. Alexander I. set a high value upon the acquisition and solemnly pledged himself to preserve unchanged the religion and constitution of the country. This promise was renewed upon the accession of every succeeding Czar, and it was reaffirmed by Alexander III. The oath of fidelity subscribed by the Finns in 1800 has always been observed to the letter by the inhabitants of the Grand Duchy, and nowhere in the Rus-

[1] Leroy-Beaulieu.

sian Empire was there to be found a people more loyal and law-abiding. Finland was the only part of the Empire where the people had any considerable rights of local self-government. The result was that up to the time of the accession of Alexander III. the growth and prosperity of Finland were phenomenal. Its population increased rapidly. Its manufactures in 1876 were twelve times as great as in 1851; in 1882 its trade returns were six times as great as in 1850.

But a manifesto put forth by Alexander III. " to form a closer union with the Grand Duchy," shattered much of this prosperity and destroyed the contentment of the people. The stable monetary system of Finland was upset by the forced introduction of the Russian paper ruble at a value determined by the Russian Minister of Finance; arbitrary Russian custom-house methods disorganized trade and manufactures; the postal system was turned over to Russian officials, who so abused their power of intercepting letters that confidential communications could not be sent by mail. The members of the Finnish Senate were compelled to resign in consequence of an official note from the Governor-General, in which the Czar's will was declared to be supreme, and the Senate was directed to subordinate itself to the orders of the Russian government.

It is evident that no promise to his subjects will bind the autocrat.

CHAPTER X.

CONCLUSION.

WHILE the present Czar has not relaxed nor substantially modified the iniquities of autocratic rule, and while his intrigues in China show that he is animated by the same spirit of conquest as his predecessors, he has startled the world and won the support of much of its unthinking philanthropy by his proposition for a partial disarmament —a proposition couched in language expressing a disinterested desire for peace. Let us consider the effect of such disarmament upon the relative prospects of Russia and the remaining powers of Europe. To illustrate, let us suppose that each of the great powers should reduce its fleets and its armies to half their present size. A few moments' consideration will show that Russia would be the gainer and England the loser by such an arrangement.

Russia's first aim is China. Her present military force would be quite unnecessary for the conquest of that empire; even the trifling armament of Japan has proven itself sufficient. Moreover it would be impossible for Russia to send any vast body of men across Siberia before the completion of the trans-Siberian Railway, which is still

some years in the future.   In the meantime she must
gain what she can by intrigue and corruption at the imperial court of Pekin, aided by the comparatively small
bodies of troops now in the vicinity, and small detach-
ments which can be gradually dispatched to Manchuria,
keeping England off in the meantime from any active
aggression by sea or across the Burmese frontier.   What
would be more useful for this purpose than peaceful
protestations and suggestions of disarmament ?   Russia
already possesses the two important seaports of the Liao-
Tung peninsula, commanding the approach to the Chinese
capital.   She must fortify these and consolidate her
power in Manchuria before she can safely move forward
by force of arms, for she could not at this moment cope
with the forces which Great Britain could send by sea
into China.   So she must wait, and if in the meantime
John Bull can be induced to diminish his navy, so much
the better.   If Russia reduces her army she can in a few
months raise it again to its present footing; if Great
Britain reduces her navy, it will take many years to restore it to its present condition.   Therefore let us dis-
arm!

It is against her Western neighbors, especially against
the Triple Alliance, that Russia keeps afoot her enormous
military establishment.   If each of these nations will
reduce its army pro-rata, she will be relatively in as good
a condition against these neighbors as she is to-day, and
the danger of an unprovoked invasion of her vast territory, with the Russian winter for her ally, is very remote.

Moreover the great armament of Russia cripples her

powers of production more than does that of any of the other nations. She needs a little time to recuperate before the final struggle. What better than a few years' truce ? In the meantime if some of her neighbors will seize each other by the ears, if England will happily get into trouble with France or Germany or America, then will come Russia's opportunity, and the Chinese Empire with its infinitely productive treasures will become her prey. Let no man blindly trust that a despotism whose history is reeking with deceit, iniquity, and outrage, is to be the Messiah of a new Gospel of Peace on earth and good will to all the nations.

By every lover of freedom the Russian autocracy must be regarded as the common enemy of all mankind.

To all nations that stand for civil liberty—nay to all men who take thought for the future of humanity—the duty is imperative to join together and stay the aggressions of the colossal empire whose conquests threaten more lasting calamity to the essentials of our civilization than did the irruption of the barbarian hordes to the civilization of ancient Rome; an empire whose universal dominion will bring into history the Dark Ages of the future—ages tenfold more hopeless than those out of which Europe has for many centuries been struggling toward the light.

Our interest in the Eastern Question may seem remote. We are so far from the scene of the struggle that it looks to us as though the consequences could never reach us. But if the Eastern continent, containing nearly the whole population of the globe, should become subject to the iron yoke of autocratic rule, would this be the end ? Would there be any limit to the aggressions of despotism ? We may be sure that no friendship with an autocrat will long protect us from final conquest, if he becomes omnipotent. The reward of our fidelity will be that which was promised by the Cyclops to Ulysses: " Him will I eat last in the number of his fellows, and the rest before him. That shall be his gift."

Most valuable perhaps of the fruits of our war with Spain has been the strengthening of the ties between ourselves and the one country of the old world that was capable of recognizing our motives for the struggle—the one country with which we ought to be united by bonds of sympathy and common interest, as well as of blood, language, and common institutions. England and America are now warm friends. Now is the golden moment to see that this friendship is made permanent and indissoluble. Let us not shrink from the union that is open to us with the most enlightened, the most humane, and the most faithful of the great powers of the earth. The warning of Washington against entangling alliances was not intended to prevent the cementing of such a union, in such a cause, and at such a period in our history. It may be wise to keep the child at home, safe from the contamination and dangers of the street, but after the boy has become a man, he must fight his battle in the world, and isolation is no longer desirable nor possible.

England once stood at our side in defending the Western hemisphere against the encroachments of the " Holy Alliance." Let us now be ready to do our part for the protection of our common civilization. The mere existence of an Anglo-American alliance will go far to remove the dangers against which it is directed.

Let us unite with England in insisting, not merely that Chinese markets shall be open to every nation upon equal terms,—not merely that the future arteries of Chinese commerce shall be controlled by those who will uphold this policy of the "open door,"—but also that not another foot of Chinese territory shall ever be ceded to Russia or to any of the allies of Russia; and not only in China, but wherever our arm extends, let us take our place by the side of England in the forefront of the struggle for the preservation of liberty throughout the world.

Sociology.

Social Facts and Forces.

The Factory—The Labor Union—The Corporation—
The Railway—The City—The Church. By WASH-
INGTON GLADDEN, author of·"Applied Christianity,"
"Tools and the Man," etc.   12°, $1.25.

"The book is full of invigorating thought, and is to be recommended to every
one who feels the growing importance of public duties."—*The Outlook*.

Socialism and the Social Movement in the Nineteenth Century.

By WERNER SOMBART, University of Breslau. Germany.
Translated by ANSON P. ATTERBURY.   With Intro-
duction by JOHN B. CLARK, Professor of Political
Economy in Columbia University.   12°, $1.25.

"Sombart's treatise on socialism impresses me as admirable; and the translation
is certainly an excellent piece of work."—J. B. CLARK, Professor of Political
Economy in Columbia University.

The Sphere of the State,

or, The People as a Body Politic.   By FRANK S. HOFF-
MAN, A.M., Professor of Philosophy, Union College.
Second edition.   12°, $1.50.

"Professor Hoffman has done an excellent piece of work. He has furnished
the student with a capital text-book and the general reader, who is interested in
political science, with much that is suggestive, much that is worthy of his careful
attention."

Anarchism.

A Criticism and History of the Anarchist Theory.   By
E. V. ZENKER.   12°, $1.50.

"The fullest and best account of anarchism ever published. . . . A most
powerful and trenchant criticism."—*London Book Gazette*.

G. P. PUTNAM'S SONS, New York & London.

Economics.

Hadley's Economics.

An Account of the Relations between Private Property and Public Welfare. By ARTHUR TWINING HADLEY, Professor of Political Economy, in Yale University. 8°, $2.50 *net*.

The work is now used in classes in Yale, Princeton, Harvard, Amherst, Dartmouth, Bowdoin, Vanderbilt, Bucknell, Bates, Leland Stanford, University of Oregon, University of California, etc.

"The author has done his work splendidly. He is clear, precise, and thorough. . . . No other book has given an equally compact and intelligent interpretation."—*American Journal of Sociology.*

The Bargain Theory of Wages.

By JOHN DAVIDSON, M A., D Phil. (Edin.), Professor of Political Economy in the University of New Brunswick. 12mo, $1.50.

A Critical Development from the Historic Theories, together with an examination of Certain Wages Factors : the Mobility of Labor, Trades Unionism, and the Methods of Industrial Remuneration.

Sociology.

A Treatise. By JOHN BASCOM, author of "Æsthetics," "Comparative Psychology," etc. 12°, $1.50.

"Gives a wholesome and inspiring word on all the living social questions of the day ; and its suggestions as to how the social life of man may be made purer and truer are rich with the finer wisdom of the time. The author is always liberal in spirit, generous in his sympathies, and wise in his knowledge."—*Critic.*

A General Freight and Passenger Post.

A Practical Solution of the Railroad Problem. By JAMES L. COWLES. Third revised edition, with additional material. 12°, cloth, $1.25 ; paper, 50 cts.

" The book gives the best account which has thus far been given in English of the movement for a reform in our freight and passenger-tariff policy, and the best arguments in favor of such reform."—EDMUND J. JAMES, in the *Annals of Political and Social Science.*

"The book treats in a very interesting and somewhat novel way of an extremely difficult subject and is well worth careful reading by all students of the transportation question." — From letter of EDW. A. MOSELEY, Secretary of the Interstate Commerce Commission, Washington, D.C.

G. P. PUTNAM'S SONS, New York & London.

www.ingramcontent.com/pod-product-compliance
Lightning Source LLC
Chambersburg PA
CBHW021128020726
47500CB00003B/977